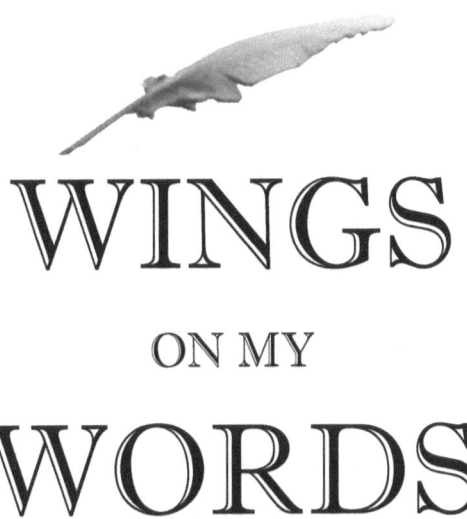

WINGS

ON MY

WORDS

TOSH MCINTOSH

Cover design and composite image: Tosh McIntosh
Front cover image: Laura Nubuck via stock.exchng
Back cover image: DNY59 via iStockphoto
Chapter graphic: BWCNY via Wikipedia Commons

For *Pilot Error* excerpt:
Cover design and composite image: Tosh McIntosh
Background cover image: Jon Sullivan
Airplane image: Jason Rainsford

ISBN-13 9781477415276
ISBN-10 1477415270

Printed in the United States of America

ACKNOWLEDGMENTS

The author wishes to express his deep appreciation to the friends and fellow writers who so graciously offered their time, expertise, and support during the conceptualization and implementation of his goal to follow the publication of his first novel with Book One of a non-fiction series on a personal writer's journey.

A special thanks to Ann Katherine McIntosh for her unfailing encouragement to never quit writing and keep my eyes on the goal.

DEDICATION

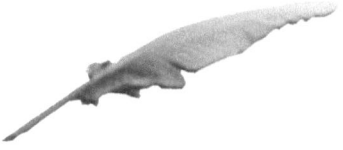

To my father, who by his quiet, gentle example, taught me the value of dedication and perseverance in pursuit of any aspiration. None of his articles or short stories were ever published, but that didn't prevent him from filling two loose leaf binders with carbon copies of submissions to the popular magazines of the day. Turning those flimsy pages, reading the words my father wrote, planted the seed of a writer without either of us recognizing it.

Rest in peace, Dad.

CONTENTS

Author's Foreword

As a career aviator, I've always embraced the philosophy that to quit learning is to tempt far more than fate. I haven't yet flown a perfect flight and I never will. Constantly striving to do better pays dividends in so many ways, and the day I don't feel like doing that will be the day I hang up my wings.

I suppose it's in the natural order of my universe to bring the same attitude from the cockpit to the writing desk. Luckily, mistakes sitting in this chair don't typically result in serious bodily injury or death, but that's no reason to accept anything less than the best I can do at any stage of my writer's journey.

This little book is the first of a series with tales from my writing desk that emphasize the role of perseverance in pursuit of the marvelous endeavor of creative writing. And while I make no claims as to their instructional value, I believe these pages contain valuable practical and motivational takeaways for anyone contemplating the task of writing a first novel.

I hope you will continue reading and ultimately agree.

One-The Seed

*All writers start the journey from a place that is
personal to them.
Write for your own reasons, not someone else's.
Stories begin with the seed of an idea.
Like pollen, seeds are everywhere.*

Seed [noun]: *a flowering plant's unit of reproduction, capable of developing into another such plant;* figurative: *the cause or latent beginning of a feeling, process or condition.*

From the dictionary, let's borrow the figurative meaning to describe what happens to the unfortunate soul who decides to write a novel.

How hard can it be? Sit down and let it flow, right?

I'm reminded of a joke about that.

The scene is a large New Year's Eve party. Guests mill around within the crowd, drinking, nibbling on hors d'oeuvres, chatting, most with the intent of winning at one-upsmanship, wearing their self-centeredness like a cloak.

Near the entrance to the room, we find two men who just arrived and haven't yet spotted someone they know. Scanning the crowd, they look for a familiar face and end up eyeball to eyeball. After introductions and a bit of small talk, the inevitable question arises about how each of them happens to know the hosts, and the conversation soon shifts to another predestined topic.

"What do you do?" asks the first man.

"I'm a physician."

"That's great. Family practice?"

"Brain surgeon."

"Wow."

"How about you?" asks the surgeon.

"I'm a writer.'

"Hmm. I've always wanted to write a novel. I may take a year off to do that, get an agent and publish it."

"Good luck with that."

"Thanks. Made any New Year's resolutions?"

"Only one."

"And that is?"

"Take a year off, go to med school and become a brain surgeon."

And, as you might imagine, the two men soon part company.

It's an old joke underpinned by an unequivocal message. Writing a novel is easy only if you've never tried it.

Many of my fellow writers have described their early childhood interest in writing. By comparison, my decision to write a novel came much later in life, a delayed sprouting of a tiny seed planted in my subconscious.

Our living room connected with my mother's studio where she taught piano. On either side of the studio door, floor-to-ceiling bookshelves contained my parents' collection of the classics, and among them sat two loose-leaf binders filled with carbon copies of articles and short stories my father submitted to the popular magazines of the 1940s and 50s.

I have no recollection of him talking about his writing. It was just something he did without fanfare in the background of our family life. The stories seemed to appear in the binders all by themselves, and I can remember sitting on the couch in the living room and reading the words my father wrote.

He kept the rejection letters there as well. They had to have been disappointing, but he never mentioned them, at least in my presence. Throughout my childhood, the binders slowly filled, providing mute witness to the perseverance of a writer who refused to give up.

And of all the lessons my father taught me by his example, advice, and counsel, this has to be the cornerstone of his life philosophy: anything worth doing in life is worth doing well, and for most of us, success requires unwavering dedication and persistence. To accept less is to cheat yourself even more than those who depend on you.

Few of us can do everything equally well. Throughout my schooling I struggled with math, physics, and chemistry. Writing always seemed naturally easy, and during my career in the United States Air Force, I had the reputation of producing quality position papers, briefings, and weapons and tactics manuals. That expertise had a profound effect on the latter stage of my career when I was selected to be the editor of the *Fighter Weapons Review,* the professional journal of the USAF Fighter Weapons Instructor School at Nellis AFB, Nevada.

After retirement from the Air Force, I flew for Continental Airlines at a time when a number of factors in the airline industry trapped me near the bottom of the seniority list. The defining characteristic of my trips was inefficiency, with a low ratio of paid time in the cockpit to total time spent on the trip. I felt like a bystander, watching countless hours of my life pass me by while I sat in airport crew rooms or layover hotels.

In the early '90s I'd had enough. But rather than quit the airline, I decided to purchase a laptop and use my sit time for something other than wasting heartbeats. Initially, I intended to do my finances, write letters, and try a little writing. One day of computer shopping reordered my objectives.

A salesman pointed out that our primary communication with a computer occurs not with the keyboard, but between our eyes and the screen. He handed me a floppy disk and suggested that I begin with the first computer in the row of laptops, type a few pages of text, copy the file to the disk and view it on each of the models.

To this day I can't remember making the decision about what to write. It could have just as easily been random letters and nonsensical words for the purpose at hand. But for whatever reason, I wrote a sentence, then another, and soon I realized that I had begun a story. I brought that floppy disk home with my new laptop.

In retrospect, if I had been the writer at that New Year's Eve party and had made the decision to take a sabbatical from writing, it would have taken less time to become the butt of that joke: Dr. Tosh McIntosh, *Brain Surgeon*.

Two-First Novel

Write what you know.
Write what you learn about.
Whatever the topic, care about it and write with passion.
Never forget the most important question: "What if . . .?"

Some writers think the secret to good stories is to infuse fiction with specific personal expertise. And while it seems obvious that a criminal trial lawyer should be better equipped to pen a legal thriller than a school teacher, what is most apparent might well lead us into a quandary. How are we to explain the commercial success of insurance salesman Tom Clancy with his techno-thrillers?

This may be nothing more than urban legend, but after the publication of *The Hunt for Red October,* Clancy supposedly received a visit from the FBI, who wanted to know where he got all the details about the operation of nuclear submarines. He replied by picking up a telephone and setting it in the middle of his desk, with the comment something to the effect of, "This is the only research tool a writer needs."

I have no idea whether that occurred or not, but the salient point is exponentially more relevant today.

In my case, decades of personal experience in aviation provided a ready-made platform for a book and an outlet for sharing with others my fascination with the world of flight. And since I had no interest in writing a memoir, my first novel began with the objective of using a fictional character to tell the story of a pilot's career in stages, described as follows:

Stage 1: *That looks like fun. I want to be a pilot.*

Stage 2: *Learning to fly an airplane is so cool! I can hardly wait to be a real pilot.*

Stage 3: *I am God's gift to aviation and therefore bulletproof.*

Stage 4: *What a blast. I wish I could still do that.*

I do not remember my choice of the story time frame for *Oasis* as being a conscious decision. The file on the floppy disk from the computer store effectively did that for me with the first two pages of a scene in which a teenager is running down the corridor of a space station being pursued by a "robodog." That probably sounds as strange to you now as it still does to me, but there you have it.

Building a story concept around this beginning resulted in a novel best described as future fiction, whose major characteristics are: 50-75 years in the future; pre- or post-apocalyptic; earth-based or barely interstellar; and advanced but recognizable technology. Here's the backstory scenario:

Years of man's abuse of the environment have taken their toll on the ability of the earth to support an ever-increasing population, and competition for life-sustaining food and water has created a have-and-have-not division among nations. The United States is in better shape than any other country, and has had to close its borders to immigration in an attempt to preserve its dwindling natural resources. American society has responded by descending rapidly into a state approaching anarchy, in which basic survival has become the vision of the future.

When the failed world economy forced all the other nations collaborating on the International Space Station to back out, the U.S. government dramatically increased NASA's budget allocation with a new objective: put a space station in orbit around the Moon to support construction of a biosphere on the lunar surface capable of indefinitely sustaining human life. As a result, the U.S. space program has emerged as the symbol of escape from impending doom, and other nations view it with covetous eyes as what may become the only true path to survival of the species.

The staggering logistical problem of transporting tons of supplies and building materials to the moon's surface dictates indefinite tours of duty on U.S. Space Station *Oasis* and Moon Colony #1. Unable to rotate scientists and mission specialists, NASA allows families and favors adult couples with relevant expertise. Children are allowed, but only one per family, and a strict birth-control policy is rigidly enforced. But as a result of unique circumstances, one couple become parents of the only human ever conceived and born in space.

The novel begins when the boy is 13 years old. He is a loner, isolated from his contemporaries because he's never been to earth. All the other children treat him like a freak. In addition, his unique origins have endowed him with sensory perceptions that exceed those of normal humans, further reinforcing his sense of not belonging.

Self-sufficient and studious beyond his years, the boy becomes infatuated with aviation and decides he wants to be a Space Command pilot. But his vision of the future is shattered when he learns that no one can learn to fly an airplane in space. Unwilling to accept the harsh reality of his situation, he decides to change it. He will convince his parents to help him obtain permission to go to earth, live with relatives, and pursue his dream.

Of all the obstacles in his path, none appears insurmountable until a single catastrophic event threatens to trap him in space forever. Unwilling to accept his fate, he vows to help save *Oasis* and Moon Colony #1 from a takeover by sinister forces intent upon auctioning long-term survival to the highest bidders.

So began the first novel in the *Oasis* series.

THREE-THE ADVENTURE BEGINS

Learn the craft.
Don't get stuck in revision limbo.
Balance reading for voice, reading to learn, and writing.

On Friday, July 30, 1993, with my brand-new laptop a constant companion on every trip, I began writing the story of a 13-year-old boy who lives on a space station, dreams of becoming a pilot, and through a confluence of unfortunate circumstances is forced to fight not only for his survival, but also that of the U.S. space program and ultimately the long-term viability of the human race.

At every opportunity, I wrote something: an hour sitting in a crew room in Houston, two hours in Cleveland, the better part of the waking hours during an overnight layover in Newark. I'd been hard at it for about three months when I happened to be sitting in the terminal in Houston waiting to board a flight home to Austin for a few days off. I had my laptop open, trying to finish up a chapter, when another Continental pilot plopped down beside me.

It turned out that he had written a novel, and his agent was in the process of auctioning the manuscript to publishers. At the time, I had no clue as to how rare that was, but it wouldn't have mattered much after he dropped a live grenade in my carefully laid authorial plans.

The explosion sounded something like this: "You know, don't you, that agents will quit reading your submission if within the first ten pages or so they don't see evidence that you have mastered the structural elements of modern fiction."

I remember smiling, nodding. *Of course.* And as soon as I arrived home, I set out to turn that falsehood into the truth.

The writer-pilot had mentioned a specific reference book. Convinced that it would be required reading for at least one creative writing course, I visited a library at the University of Texas. Three copies were listed in the card catalog, one of which I found deep within the stacks. It had been published in the 1930s, last checked out five years prior, and finding it left me with a profound sense of having misunderstood what the other pilot had said. No way would an essential reference book not have more recent publication dates and be so unused.

One visit to a bookstore close to the campus presented the opposite problem: so many books and no idea how to choose. I finally settled on the *Elements of Fiction* series by Writers' Digest Books, bought the volumes they had in stock and ordered the rest.

And that introduced another problem. Should I stop writing and read about how I'm supposed to be doing it, forget about learning to write from a book and just write, or compromise and do some of both? After scanning the contents of a book or two in the series, I decided to compromise. For every hour spent writing, I'd spend an hour reading.

In retrospect, this method proved to be an effective combination of analytical precision and unleashed imagination. My pilot's brain could flow with creativity anywhere, even outside the box.

And that process introduced yet another problem. Should I return to the beginning of the novel and begin revising based on having learned something new, or keep on writing? One of the first reference books I read mentioned the circular revision syndrome and how it can unnecessarily prolong and even prevent a writer from completing a first draft. I elected to forge ahead by devoting equal time to both objectives.

Another bit of advice reinforced that approach: write every scene for everything it's worth and don't worry about word count. This encourages writers to treat first drafts as a good cook handles a sauce. An early taste will be disappointing because the ingredients have not yet had the time to meld. But once the sauce has been carefully simmered, a process one book called "distilling," the reduction gains complexity and character that can never be achieved by rushing the process.

Being on the road about 18-20 days per month left little time at home to deal with the demands of maintaining the homestead and my cars (I had three at the time, none less than two decades old). That meant I wrote only when on trips, which in a strange way helped me deal with the frustrations of commuting to work and airline flying. I seldom looked forward to work periods, but always eagerly anticipated a return to the world of my story and discovering what was going to happen next.

Under these conditions, the first draft consumed about two years of effort and produced an enormous word count. At the time, I knew nothing about submitting the manuscript to agents and did not appreciate the importance of having a target word count depending on genre and the fact that I was an unpublished author.

Oasis in first draft clocked in at 484,000 words. For those of you who know about word count guidelines, that's not a typo. At the standard word count per printed page, this equates to a book of almost 2000 pages. Try holding that monster in your lap, and don't even think about carrying it on a trip.

Oblivious to the bloated, overweight condition of my first draft, I eagerly began the next phase, the all-important step of following more advice on how to write a novel: *revise, revise, and revise some more.*

Four-The Big No Thanks

Learn the rules.
Don't submit prematurely.
Prepare for disappointment.
Don't take rejection personally.
The only preordained path to failure is to quit.

With my behemoth first draft divided into four parts simply as a way of making it easier to handle, and having read all my how-to books from cover to cover, I began revising the novel. Over the next two years, still writing almost exclusively on the road, I had completed the fifth draft and accomplished the amazing (or so I thought) feat of reducing the word count by 25%. I'll do the math for you: that's about 365,000 words remaining.

There's a saying that it's sometimes not what you know but whom. It just so happened that two of my friends were acquainted with people in the publishing industry, and both offered to introduce me. Totally oblivious to how premature this effort was, I sent the novel to an editor and an agent with the naive expectation that this would turn out to be my big break. The agent replied with a kindly worded rejection that the novel didn't fit with his current interests, and the editor ignored me.

Neither result provided anything useful, like pointing out that *Oasis* was 3.5 times the recommended maximum for a book by an unpublished author.

I continued learning the details of submitting to agents and bought two more books on how to choose the agents I wanted to query from a list of a few hundred members of the Association of Author's Representatives, and how to write the all-important query letter and a companion synopsis.

This preparation effort took forever and revealed to me a truth that is still accurate today: I'd rather be faced with an engine failure on an airplane than have to write a query letter. But I finally had the package ready and set about assembling hard copies for each of the agents to be sent via snail mail.

Mailing five per week was my goal, which took about ten weeks. The results were not pretty: 40 form rejections, five no replies, and five were undeliverable as addressed. With my pen so rudely capped, I retreated into a world of glum self-pity and thought seriously about giving up.

If I've learned anything, this initial experience dealing with rejection has probably been the most difficult obstacle. I can't even begin to count the number of times I've stopped writing and simply walked away from it with no thought of returning.

But like a glowing ember in the ashes, the desire to tell a story that someone might enjoy reading waits patiently for a tiny bit of kindling.

And that's a good thing, because the only true path to failure is to quit.

Five-Wanna Write a Mystery?

Join a writers' group.
Develop, refine, and perfect your writing style.
Find a compatible book doctor to mentor your learning.
Consider targeting the center of a popular genre.
Write from an organized plan to develop a layered plot and
an engaging main character.

L ost in a writer's wilderness of no confidence, I called the offices of the Writers' League of Texas (WLT) and asked to speak with someone who might help me decide where to turn next. At the time, a published author with a number of books, short stories, and articles to his credit volunteered at the WLT office. He answered the phone, listened to my plea for help and offered the following four suggestions:

First, join a writers' critique group.

Second, find a compatible editor to mentor my learning.

Third, as an unpublished author, consider aiming directly for the center of an established, popular genre.

Fourth, the largest section of any bookstore is devoted to mysteries, so why not write one?

"And," he said, "I'm teaching a course this weekend on how to write a mystery. Should I sign you up?"

Armed with notes from his course, the experience of writing a massive mess of a novel behind me, and having read all my how-to books, I began developing the concept for a mystery series.

The course had emphasized the importance of the main character's (MC) role as a disenfranchised sleuth. He's either currently in law enforcement, or more commonly used to be, and one of his opponents is another cop (senior to the MC) who hates his guts and is looking for any justification to make his life miserable.

Then there's the sidekick, usually the MC's partner (or ex-partner), who tries to help the MC in any way he can without getting himself fired.

The MC lives in a no man's land between law enforcement by the book, all nice and legal, and the attitude of *whatever it takes*. But the motivation for this extra-legal activity isn't for personal gain or blood lust. It's all about justice for the victims, especially when the legal approach can't touch the bad guy, who is going to avoid prosecution if the MC doesn't do something to stop it.

One of my favorite characters in mystery fiction, a homicide detective, is shown in a long scene committing a felony (breaking and entering). He knows who the killer is, but he can't prove it, and he's convinced that incriminating evidence is hidden in the killer's residence. Without a search warrant, that's where it will stay unless the cop takes the matter into his own hands.

The scene shows all the details from casing the house, the approach, the entry, the initial search in all the most common places, followed by a more through examination, all under the pressure of a ticking clock. He spends no more than a preset amount of time in the house, then he's out of there.

Illegal? Absolutely. Justified? Absolutely again. And I think most mystery readers would agree. This is the long arm of justice reaching out to dispense punishment on those who commit acts so horrific that forgiveness isn't an option. It also counteracts the legal system's emphasis on protecting the accused and thereby further victimizing the innocent.

Initially I planned the series around a cop/private investigator, but the theme of aviation from *Oasis* quickly altered my objective. As is true with most fiction, it began with a few simple questions.

What if an aviation accident investigator discovers evidence of criminal wrongdoing in the wreckage of an airplane? And what if, during the search for who committed the sabotage, the investigator has to step way outside his official authority to bring a killer to justice? And what if, as a result, he is no longer employed as an accident investigator? And what if he becomes a private crash detective?

With that concept as a starting point, I developed a rough plot line, list of characters and settings, and began writing. Thirty-two days later, I had completed an 84,000-word novel, *Pilot Error*. And when I got to the last page, the realization that the story had reached a finale took me by surprise. I almost couldn't believe it.

The only explanation I've been able to come up with is that I'd already made one of the most common beginner mistakes on *Oasis*. I'd lost my way, headed down blind plot alleys while losing sight of the core story in an orgy of word over-indulgence.

It had begun in a computer store by letting my mind run with an idea but without a leash. And since then, I've learned that while some writers may be able to create stories that work in an environment unfettered by the constraints of a plan, an outline, a synopsis, or whatever you choose to call it, I work best with structure from the very beginning.

Writers sometimes tell me this is writing "by the numbers." I can see their point and acknowledge the opinion. On the other hand, over the years of involvement in critique groups, I've seen far more examples of rudderless drifting in plot doldrums than I have of tracking a course toward a satisfying destination.

My mystery novel in first draft, however, even if restrained by word frugality, had a long journey ahead to put the right words in the right places.

SIX-SIMMERING THE SAUCE

Learn which advice to ignore.
Learn which advice to incorporate right now.
Learn which advice to hold for further consideration.
Above all, avoid revision limbo.

There may be writers out there who can create a story that works in first draft. If so, I'll have to envy them from afar, because I don't know any and I'm pretty certain I never will.

I'm also certain that every how-to book on writing stresses the importance of revising. In the *Oasis* chapters, I mentioned one source that likened revising to reducing a sauce, and the analogy is a good one. If that's the goal, how does a writer best go about it?

When I began the second draft of *Pilot Error*, one salient objective hijacked my efforts. The culprit was another bit of advice about how to avoid the circular revision syndrome mentioned in Chapter Three. The condition creates a word eddy that can prevent a writer from completing a first draft. Here's an example.

Let's say I'm in the middle of chapter seven in first draft and find that some element of the story has drifted off course.

The most common response is to stop right there, return to the beginning of the novel, and revise earlier chapters as necessary so they reflect the new direction up to chapter seven.

The problem with this approach is that it invariably will happen more than once, and each time, the writer's efforts won't be restricted to a single story element. With every revision that starts at the beginning, additional changes continue to affect the story. It's a word eddy that can easily trap a writer indefinitely.

The preventative measure is to list the changes for the earlier chapters and keep on writing. When the first draft is done, the list will have grown and can be addressed on a true second draft of the entire novel and not just an unfinished portion. I religiously followed that advice, and the resulting list dominated my efforts with the second draft. But that's not all.

By this point I had joined a writers' critique group. With a completed novel in revision, I had the opportunity to submit 100 pages in four installments during my first year of participation. These roundtable discussions provided me with additional items to consider for subsequent revisions.

To keep track of the various drafts, I began using a version-number system and soon realized that I needed a way to indicate the degree to which a subsequent version differed from the previous one, similar to software upgrades: v3, v3.1, v4, etc.

Some writers feel that you can revise too much. In my experience, the problem is usually expressed as editing out all the soul from the writing and making it sterile. I'm not sure I agree, but there's another revision trap that might be even worse: attempting to satisfy everyone else in a writers' group.

Critique group participation is a topic worthy of a chapter all its own (the next one). At this point in my journey, I hadn't yet learned how to evaluate the relative validity of individual comments. That endowed them all equally, and the result was a confused compromise that didn't reflect the suggestions or my vision of the story. No one could claim ownership.

I learned a lot about writing during this period and the novel improved, but never to the point that I felt it had reached its true potential.

Through the Writers' League of Texas, I contacted a local freelance editor. We agreed that I would submit the entire novel in installments of about 40 pages each. My objective for this collaboration was to submit, receive her critique, incorporate the suggestions in the material, then revise the next 40 pages with those lessons in mind and submit them. The measure of my success was very simple: to steadily reduce the number of corrections/suggestions and increase the happy faces.

And that's what happened. By the time we reached the last installment, I received the best report card to date and concluded that I was once again ready to submit to agents.

As you might have guessed, I was wrong.

But before I tell you about that revolting development, let's talk about . . .

Seven–Writers' Groups

To group, or not to group, that is the question.
Some writers are totally incompatible with any group.
Mutual-admiration-society (fluff) groups are worthless.
No group is compatible with all writers who choose to
participate in one.
If you join, leave your ego at home, wear your thick skin to
the meetings, stick with it long enough to develop a com-
ment filter that works for you, and do your best to give and
receive with equal dedication to the collaborative effort.
Most of you will be glad you did.

Each writer has to determine whether a group serves a useful function. Is participation worth the time and effort? To answer that question requires considering two more basic issues.

Should writers *ever* discuss their novels with anyone? Does outside input pollute a manuscript in some fundamental way? If your answer is, "No," then what about waiting until the first draft is complete before placing the manuscript in front of others?

Some writers believe that participation in novel-*in-progress* groups is a flawed effort, and we should consider them to be novel-*in-revision* groups in both name and function. And although it may seem to be a question of semantics, for me the distinction isn't so easily dismissed.

To begin working on a manuscript is like spinning a cocoon around me and the writing desk. If I can't enter the fictive dream and become lost in the fictional world of my characters, how can I expect the words I write to accomplish that for the reader?

The operative concept here is the word **solitary**: adjective: *done or existing alone; secluded or isolated; lonely, companionless, unaccompanied, by oneself, on one's own, alone, friendless; antisocial, unsociable, withdrawn, reclusive, cloistered, hermitic, incommunicado, lonesome.* I've provided a definition and synonyms to emphasize the nuances of experience inherent in the challenge of telling a story that works.

For me, writing and revising a novel with the assistance of a critique group has been well worth the commitment of time and effort required. That said, *Pilot Error* was complete before I joined the group. The first draft of the sequel *Red Line*, however, is currently in progress, and I believe that the critiques of others are making it a better novel than it otherwise would be.

Some personal observations from years at the roundtable:

Groups have a communal personality. Like any social entity, they change over time.

Egos have to be left at home. Once a writer begins taking comments personally, benefit suffers.

Writers need to find a group compatible with their personality and interests. Depending on where you live, this can be impossible or relatively easy. No group close by? Start one, and remember in the world of the Internet, you don't have to write in a vacuum.

Roundtable discussions appear at first glance to be the heart of any group, when in reality the outside associations that develop provide the most benefit. Identifying a few writers in the group as critique buddies with whom you can trade material on a regular basis is an effective way to be reviewed more frequently.

Participation requires commitment to the idea that each of us learns by both acting as reviewers and being reviewed, because you will spend more time evaluating other writers' material than vice versa. In my experience, the benefits of reviewing flow from two distinctly different aspects of the roundtable.

First, everyone at the table has read the same submission. In almost every meeting, one or more members will comment on something I didn't notice. Each of these tidbits can become part of my craft, and the lessons learned have generally proven to be at least as valuable as being critiqued.

Second, reviewing manuscripts outside of my personal reading and writing interests forces me out of my comfort zone. And while some writers think that diminishes the value of a critique, I believe many structural elements of fiction transcend genre. If my review objective is to analyze how well a submission reflects common structure, unfamiliarity with the content and unique elements of another genre is no excuse for not doing my best to offer something worthy of another writer's consideration.

Roundtable comments by reviewers fall into three basic categories:

- Right-on, you know it immediately.
- Way off, you toss it out as being so far off base that it isn't worth considering
- In the middle somewhere, you let it percolate and over time determine how much of it you will incorporate.

Roundtable comments also vary by how often you hear them:

- Some are offered only once, receive no support from other members of the group, and are often the ones easiest to reject.
- But one member can also see something no one else does, and it becomes an item you immediately accept as right on because it needs no supporting opinion.
- Unanimous comments are hard to reject because if the group is good enough to stay with, widely held opinions carry the weight of authority that you have already accepted as beneficial by participating.

Eight–Another Big No Thanks

From my friend and fellow writer Brad Whittington:
"On agents at conferences: Just because the waitress is
friendly doesn't mean she's into you."
"It's a lesson from pop music. Unlike jazz, where the
audience will give you a few verses to get rolling,
you have to burn from the first bar."

With the novel freshly revised by incorporating the suggestions of a professional editor, I signed up for the Writers' League of Texas yearly agents' conference and entered the manuscript contest. It didn't take long to receive two shots of writer's adrenaline.

The first was when I learned that I'd made finalist in the mystery/thriller category, and that winners historically receive an offer of representation from an agent.

The second heart-pumping event occurred when I heard about an attending agent who supposedly had offered representation to a bunch of unknown writers as a result of the previous year's conference. But when I tried to sign up for a one-on-one session with her, none were available.

"Do not despair," writer friends told me. "There are plenty of opportunities to pitch an agent outside of the scheduled sessions. Walking the halls of the venue, in the elevator," hence the name, 30-second elevator pitch, "or at the meet-and-greet sessions, but you have to be ready and do not hesitate. Agents entering a room of conference attendees draw a crowd faster than you can blink. If you're in the back of the pack and don't have the physique of an NFL linebacker, act like one of those shifty wide receivers and run a sneaky route."

Enter the "ambush." I armed myself with a practiced spiel sure to engage the agent's interest, studied the agent's mug shot, and scouted the venue for the most likely intercept point. The lobby of the hotel seemed logical, with a view of the welcoming desk where agents would pick up their name tags. On the Friday afternoon before the social hour that evening, I lay in wait for my victim.

Lo and behold, there she appeared, and then immediately entered a gift shop near the front door. I realize this sounds a lot like stalking, and I admit the resemblance, but my assault was strictly verbal.

After a few moments, she exited the gift shop and headed toward the staircase. Using all my skill at intercept geometry (from my days as a fighter pilot), I joined up with her right beside a huge potted plant in a small sitting area. The words that came out were totally unplanned, I suppose because my carefully prepared pitch had become lost in my grey-matter trash bin. I blurted out something to the effect of, "I hope this isn't a breach of etiquette to introduce myself before you've had the opportunity to pin on your name tag."

She smiled, always a good sign, and said, "Hold on a minute," put her briefcase down on a chair, and pinned on her nametag. "Now you're well within your rights."

I'll always remember how effectively that put me at ease. And in retrospect, her ability to do that is a major reason she was so popular among conference attendees. After a nice conversation, unhurried by the press of any other writers trying to wedge their way between us, she asked me to send her the complete manuscript of *Pilot Error* and did I have anything else ready? When I mentioned *Oasis*, she asked for that as well.

I'd been at the conference for less than an hour. To say that this made me feel as if I'd finally arrived would be an understatement. To say that I was grossly naive would be an understatement in the extreme.

At that time, manuscript contest winners in each category were announced by someone reading the first few paragraphs to the crowd at the opening meeting of the conference. The mystery/thriller category was last, of course, so I had to sit in suspense waiting for the news. And by the time the winner of the fourth category had been announced, I knew I wouldn't be walking up to the podium as the fifth winner.

And this experience taught me something very important, that from the first sentence of the first paragraph, a writer's challenge is to grab the reader's attention and interest and never let go. Listening to four winning examples highlighted for me the reality of having failed to appreciate how important that is.

But I still had the opportunity to meet one-on-one in session with an agent and intercept others in the highways and byways of the conference. I didn't realize it at the time, but generally speaking, any personal contact with an agent at a conference results in a request for material. It's the quickest way an agent can pry a writer's fingers from their arms and disengage.

I mailed all the manuscripts within a week. For all but my dream agent, they resulted in standard form rejection letters. For her, the manuscripts fell off the edge of the earth along with the agent. At the time, I heard that her marketing tactic didn't involve going directly to publishers with a manuscript, but publishing a catalog, of sorts, like, "These are the manuscripts I have, let me know if you are interested." I don't know if that's true or not, only that I never heard from her again, and rumor has it that most other writers who submitted to her didn't either.

Now I *really* wanted to give up.

And I did for a while, but the nagging urge to write something worthy of publication would not be denied.

Nine-Send Me The Full

Ignorance of the law (rule) is no excuse.
Learn structure, even if you choose to ignore it on occasion.
If this sounds like too much work, writing a novel might
not be your best choice.
Try essays, poetry, short stories . . . or gardening.

L icking the wounds of repudiation gets really tiring and works only for a limited time as an excuse for putting a writing goal aside rather than actively pursuing it. I finally decided to try again, and while four of the first five queries resulted in the all-too-familiar form rejection letters, the fifth sent a fresh supply of writer's adrenaline though my bloodstream when the agent requested a full manuscript. It's a hard-to-forget feeling.

His email said "as soon as possible," which indicated to me that this was something really special. It turned out not to be when a week later I received a rejection letter. But for the first time an agent provided reasons for not offering representation. He felt that the solution to the mystery was "too dependent upon coincidence and almost miraculous inference." I asked if he would reconsider the manuscript if I addressed the deficiencies, to which he replied, "I welcome the opportunity."

That seemed positive enough to be worth the effort. In the absence of more specific criticism, I printed the dictionary definitions of *coincidence, miraculous,* and *inference* in large type, taped them to my writing desk, and went hunting for places in the story that might have contributed to the agent's decision.

In the meantime, the local freelance editor who had helped me with an earlier version suggested that I attend a weekend workshop presented by John Truby. When I questioned the applicability of a screenwriting course to writing novels, she set me straight with the reply, "It's about story *structure,* not the medium."

The workshop experience justifies a dedicated chapter (the next one), but in summary, I came away with a different view as to what makes stories work based upon the ways a writer can encourage readers to enter the fictive dream and remain there. With the novel already in revision to address the agent's concerns, I decided to incorporate the lessons learned.

I finished the revision in three weeks with confidence that I'd significantly improved the manuscript, but without conviction that I'd addressed the agent's comments well enough to obtain representation. Despite my uncertainty, and with the hope that he would appreciate my willingness to reshape the novel and my eagerness to collaborate, I resubmitted the manuscript.

The agent's prompt response to my original submission led me to expect the same with the second. As the weeks passed, I developed an optimistic explanation: the delay meant that he was having a much harder time saying, "No." When I finally queried him as to the status, he responded with another rejection, but for entirely different reasons than the first time, and in far greater detail. The following is an edited version:

I think that you've done some terrific work here in revising it but I regret I am still not able to offer representation.

There are many factors that an agent takes into account when considering a submission, and I have thought long and hard about this story. My problem—despite your revisions—is that I feel this is still too much in the middle of the road—it's not grounded enough in reality (I find myself wishing for a stronger political grounding, more forensic science and investigative details), and not fantastic enough (I find myself wanting a better picture of this paid assassin, his master, and, finally, the man behind it all, the President).

What you have here is a good story. Unfortunately, in the current thriller market, I feel that one has to go to publishers with a great story to even get on the board. I regret that we can only offer you all our best wishes for your future success at this time.

This letter struck me as genuine from the agent's perspective and especially significant from mine for two reasons. First, it made no mention of the previous justification for not offering representation, and second, it addressed more specific problems that went to the heart of the story and its characters. Without asking if the agent would be interested in taking another look, I embarked on the most aggressive revision yet and added about 120 pages to the manuscript.

Major changes included: beefing up the reasons for the murder with deeper political motivation, expanding the roles of the assassin, his handler, and the President, and providing far more accident investigation detail. But when I queried the agent again, he declined the opportunity to reconsider the manuscript. Subsequently, I learned that agents will seldom, if ever, take a third look. What now?

My initial response was to walk away from the writing desk for a while. At moments like these, disappointment, doubt, and discouragement (alliteration intentional) threatened to derail the dream (there I go again—sorry) and it was so tempting to quit.

But if you ask any writer, you will probably hear a similar refrain, something to the effect of, "I can't *not* write." And so it was for me.

Ten-The Truby Experience

"But I'm writing a novel, not a screenplay."
"It's all about structure, Tosh, not the medium."
What a difference a three-day workshop can make.

My writing career, such as it is now or may turn out to be, from this point forward became defined in terms of before and after Truby. The learning can be divided into three categories:

- What I thought I knew, but not well enough (validation, but with enhancement).
- What I thought I knew, but was wrong about (correction).
- What I had no clue about (revelation and enlightenment, the largest of the three categories).

If asked to characterize the learning in the broadest terms, the response would be this: I knew that fiction works because it is a reflection of real life. But readers get enough of real life every day, and they don't read novels to get more of it. So the reflection needs to be magnified until it appears larger than life. Every human trait, emotion, experience, etc. needs to be enhanced. The process works because readers willingly suspend disbelief, accept what is to follow as fiction, and effectively think, *Okay, we both know this isn't real, now entertain me.*

But I didn't know *why* the process works, and how a proven method can assist me in achieving my personal goal in writing, which is to entertain. Truby's 22-step method mirrors the manner in which human beings, regardless of race, color, creed, religion, or national origin, go about the business of daily life and deal with it. If the writer can build a story upon this structure, it will reach out to readers and touch them in a fundamentally deep and basic way. This connection is what draws readers in and keeps them there.

The vast majority of stories fail because, as in any structure that must stand on its own and collapses, the writer has failed to lay the first brick well and mortar it into position. Truby taught me how to accomplish first things first, and build from there.

The method, far from being a constricting roadmap and formula defining the limits of creativity, does just the opposite. It allows me to express creativity in a much more effective fashion by guiding, not leading, the building of an internal structure upon which the story must depend.

In a nutshell, Truby offers the following tasty morsels:

Write on a piece of paper everything you ever wanted to see in a novel or on the screen: snippets of dialogue, plot lines, settings, characters, anything and everything that interests you as a reader/viewer.

Study the paper for trends, which define in general terms the essential nature of stories you like.

From these trends, develop the best premise you can, one that really excites you, and with which you can bond internally because you care about it. The premise is the first brick. The vast majority of writers cannot develop a workable premise, and this is the primary reason most stories fail in the middle and cannot sustain themselves through to the end.

Then set the frame of the story by defining the start and end points. This multiple step establishes the overall range of change of the hero, and sets the structural journey the hero takes. To set the frame:

Define the self-revelation at the end, in which the hero is stripped bare and can see who he/she really is, the true self exposed. This occurs after the crucible of battle (literally or figuratively), and is the result of the concept that "whatever doesn't kill you makes you stronger."

Establish the hero's need at the start. Need arises from a problem/difficulty the hero faces. He/she knows what it is, but not how to solve it. Need then is defined as what the hero must fulfill to have a better life, that which is missing inside the hero based on a great weakness. Needs are defined as being either psychological (strictly personal, a missing element that has no direct negative effect on anyone other than the hero), or moral (with a direct negative effect on others by hurting them, what the hero must learn to act properly toward others, and about which he/she is ignorant).

Establish the hero's desire at the start. Desire is not need. Desire is defined as a specific goal the hero wants and provides a track upon which the hero rides, what he/she cares about, wants to see accomplished. Good desire lines require motive (why hero wants it, providing the justification for action), and stakes (the goal must be valuable, because if the hero doesn't care, neither will the reader).

Define what the hero learns at the end.

Define what the hero knows at the start.

Define what the hero is wrong about at the start.

Once the frame of the story is set, begin filling in the middle by addressing each of the structural elements.

My initial experience with the process:

I purchased Truby's Blockbuster software to write the screenplay for *Pilot Error.* My purpose was twofold: have it ready for the agents who would be pounding at my door wanting to sell the screen rights (what's life if you can't dream?), and improve the novel in the process. More than one writer who has tried screenplays has told me this helped them with dialogue.

Then I realized I didn't have the time. An agent was interested in the novel. I needed to resubmit the manuscript promptly with no sidetracking.

So I "backfilled" Truby's 22 steps with *Pilot Error* to create the structural basis I might have developed if I had used it prior to completing the novel. This effort produced no fewer than ten changes that I firmly believe improved the manuscript substantially. It assisted me in identifying flaws and gave me a way to correct them. The overall process was exciting, to say the least.

Eleven—The Book Doctor

When is the right time to consider hiring a book doctor?
How can you separate the scam artists from the real deal?
How do you choose a book doctor that's a good fit for you
and your novel?
There's a big difference between content/developmental,
line, and copy editing.
Always confirm in advance exactly what you're getting
for your money.

During the years of struggling to publish a novel, milestones remain behind to mark significant turning points in my journey. And of these, the agent's declining the opportunity to look at the manuscript for a third time put me at a three-way intersection: quit, continue submitting the most recent and extensively revised version to agents, or search for a higher level of critical input than available to me locally with my critique group.

Turning again to the Writers' League of Texas, I obtained the names of three freelance editors, or book doctors, who had assisted other League members. Preliminary contact with all three left me uncertain about whether I should engage their services. Their qualifications had no bearing on my reaction.

All were experienced, with the credentials to match. But there seemed to be something missing.

Then I found a respected guide to agents, editors, and publishers with an extensive advice-to-authors section. A pair of articles on the topic of book doctors helped clarify the decision-making process by addressing a number of questions.

How do you know when the time has come to hire a book doctor? How do you avoid the scam artists? How do you identify the real deal? And most important, how do you choose a book doctor that is right for you and your novel? Of all the decisions I had to make, the last question resonated the most.

One of the articles recommended a couple of websites with the names and credentials of book doctors with reputations for providing excellent editorial services at a fair price. From two lists of about twenty different book doctors, all of whom were fully qualified and vetted, I had to choose the criteria for narrowing the field down to one.

The decision turned out to be a no-brainer. I found an editor who had worked with five nominees and one winner of the prestigious Edgar® Award, presented annually by the Mystery Writers of America. In addition, his credentials noted that he loved aviation. This had the potential for a match made in struggling-writer hell, and it's an important point. Any professional editor can help improve a manuscript, but you're looking for one whose personal reading preferences as reflected in the kinds of books he or she edits are a good match with the book you have written. If your novel is one the editor would pay to read, it stands to reason that you will receive a more comprehensive and valuable critique.

A couple of emails established the ground rules for how the initial critique would work, and what I would receive for a set cost in a defined amount of time. I engaged his services and he delivered exactly as promised: a 17-page written critique and comments inserted in the manuscript to illustrate specific concepts, both within seven weeks of initiating our agreement.

To say that the critique blew me away is no exaggeration. He made suggestions for improving both the story and the mechanics of telling it by using concepts I'd never heard of.

In trying to get a handle on the lessons contained in the critique, I began organizing the written comments into categories and quickly discovered that about 75% of his suggestions related to story structure, which I had previously thought was one of my strengths as a writer. Although not a novice, I hadn't yet grasped some of the key elements of thrillers.

And this brings up a key point that applies to working with both the agent and the editor. I set out to write a mystery.

The subject of genre definitions deserves a chapter of its own (in Book Two), but suffice it to say here that part of the agent's justification for not offering representation was because I hadn't written a novel that could compete in the current thriller market.

When I asked the editor about that, he set me straight: "It matters not what you intended to write. *Pilot Error* is a thriller." Well, okay then. What now?

Thus began a period of collaboration lasting over two years, not because it took that long to deal with the issues, but for economic reasons. Critique groups offer suggestions for free. Book doctors do not.

Using the initial critique, I revised the manuscript from start to finish. Although this effort concentrated on story structure, it also attempted to incorporate the editor's suggestions for improving my handling of other elements. I submitted the complete novel for another critique, and here's where a failure to communicate caused problems.

In retrospect, I blame both of us for the misunderstanding as to our objective for this critique. I thought he would be doing the same big-picture analysis outlined in our original discussions. But I learned otherwise when I received an email reporting that he had paused about halfway through the manuscript. I'm glad he did, and credit him with the integrity to verify that I wanted him to continue before proceeding further.

Unbeknownst to me, he was doing a close edit. To use Holly Lisle's analogy in her "How To Revise Your Novel" course, the book doctor was performing cosmetic surgery on a patient bleeding from an open wound. Time to regroup.

With the half-completed critique for reference, I began another revision with the understanding that we would adopt the same installment procedure I used with the local freelance editor. In this case, we divided the novel into thirds, agreeing that we wouldn't proceed further until the first third had passed his review. His concurrence with this method was conditional, however, in that he couldn't judge the complete novel without performing a continuous and uninterrupted evaluation.

This chapter has no tidy ending. The book doctor was reviewing the second installment when I contacted him for an update. He apologized for the delay, said that he had spent more time than planned on it, and promised to deliver the critique within a week. After waiting for over a month, I decided not to follow up.

Two factors ended our collaboration: 1) my generalized impression that while I had learned a lot and the manuscript had significantly improved, in terms of receiving additional benefit the law of diminishing return might be in play; and 2) a 50% reduction in family income due to loss of my flying job when my employer sold the airplane.

Once again, a turning point in the journey had arrived.

TWELVE-THE DOCTOR'S PRESCRIPTION

Why can't my fallacies be pathetic?
What is total characterization and how do I create it?
What's so important about keeping agency
with the human?
I decided not to take up gardening, so what's the
big deal about a budding flower?

Released from the book doctor's care by unspoken mutual agreement, I now had only his prescription for success. But as I aggressively continued with revising and submitting the results to both of my writers' groups, there were no limits on doses of three medications: *total characterization, keeping agency with the human,* and *the budding flower.* Let's look at the properties and effects of each.

Members' comments indicated what I can only describe as having turned a corner with some of the issues the editor had found troublesome in earlier manuscripts. And what struck me as especially interesting was the fact that while local, non-professional reviewers had been previously critical of the same things, they were unable to help me fix what was wrong. But now they noted the improvement and provided validation that I was on the right track.

Reviewers of early versions often commented on what they described as my failure to let them get close to the main character (MC). They wanted me to put them inside his head more. I took the criticism seriously and tried various methods to fix the problem, including more deep internalization using italicized thoughts. The first manuscript critiqued by the book doctor displayed the results of my attempts to satisfy local reviewers, and he promptly pounced on that as being poor technique.

"The best way to let readers know what a character is thinking is to effectively show what he's saying and doing. The worst way is to insert a running mental commentary to make sure readers get it." And so began the book doctor's lesson on total characterization.

Pilot Error is written in limited-multiple point-of-view (POV, or viewpoint), which means: 1) every scene is confined to the perceptions of a participating character; 2) readers can view the story from only one character's perspective within any scene; and 3) the story is told from the viewpoint of more than one character.

Writers commonly refer to a character's camera when discussing viewpoint, but this can lead to a narrowed consideration of the topic because it relates only to what the character sees. And while the vast majority of a story is presented to readers through the viewpoint character's visualization of events, the other four senses also play an important role in what is best described as getting within a character's skin.

In presenting the concept of total characterization, the book doctor added important elements to the five senses: thoughts, words, actions, perceptions, and in particular, what the character perceives and *how* the character perceives it.

To illustrate the point, he suggested that I read some of Ross MacDonald's Lew Archer series and pay particular attention to the techniques MacDonald uses to characterize the protagonist. According to the book doctor, MacDonald effectively transformed the private investigator of the '30s and '40s into a new breed that dominated the '50s and beyond.

I'm not sure I learned what the book doctor intended. The best way I can describe it is to imbue the character with attitude: *a settled way of thinking or feeling about someone or something, typically one that is reflected in a person's behavior.* Which returns us full circle to the character's words and actions as key elements of behavior and the primary window into the character's mind. Here's an example that repeats in one form or another in the three novels I read.

Archer is a gumshoe, but in MacDonald's novels, unlike those of his predecessors, the setup never begins in a seedy office, redolent with cigarette smoke, with the detective's feet propped on a desk beside an almost-empty bottle of booze and a stack of unpaid bills. Archer has already been hired, and he's making first contact with his clients in their world.

At first, it's only his camera in action describing the setting, a key element of fiction so that characters don't appear in front of a white sheet. But MacDonald carefully chooses the specifics of what Archer notices about his surroundings, and the salient point for total characterization is how he interprets that which captures his attention. Here's the opening paragraph from *The Way Some People Die:*

> *The house was in Santa Monica on a cross street between boulevards, within earshot of the coast highway and rifleshot of the sea. The street was the kind that people had once been proud to live on, but in the last few years it had lost its claim to pride. The houses had too many stories, too few windows, not enough paint. Their history was easy to guess:*

they were one-family residences broken up into apartments and light-housekeeping rooms, or converted into tourist homes. Even the palms that lined the street looked as if they had seen their best days and were starting to lose their hair.

How can a reader not be engaged by that? The second paragraph provides more details, and then this:

The house didn't look as if it had any money in it, or ever would have again. I went in anyway, because I liked the woman's voice on the phone.

That opening is so much more than setting. It endows a special flavor to the case that Archer has just taken, along with a wonderfully descriptive glimpse into the mind of the MC. And we know that Archer recognizes the signs of having fallen on harder times, probably because he's been there.

The opening two paragraphs and a bit of the third of *Black Money* present the opposite situation, Archer arriving at a location to meet a wealthy client.

I'd been hearing about the Tennis Club for years, but I'd never been inside it. Its courts and bungalows, its swimming pool and cabanas and pavilions, were disposed around a cove of the Pacific a few miles south of the Los Angeles County border. Just parking my Ford in the asphalt lot beside the tennis courts made me feel like less of a dropout from the affluent society.

The carefully groomed woman at the front desk of the main building told me that Peter Jamieson was probably in the snack bar. I walked around the end of the fifty-meter pool, which was enclosed on three sides by cabanas. On the fourth side the sea gleamed through a ten-foot wire fence like a blue fish alive in a net. A few dry bathers were lying around as if the yellow eye of the sun had hypnotized them.

When I saw my prospective client, in the sunny courtyard outside the snack bar, I recognized him instinctively. He looked like money about three generations removed from its source.

When I first read the openings of these two novels, it occurred to me that Archer's attention to these details might end up being clues to the mystery. They weren't, and they didn't have to be essential parts of the plot to serve a vital purpose. They are setting and characterization all rolled into one: what Archer notices and how he interprets it.

The book doctor noted a second ailment, an affliction I caused myself by overdose. Local author and editor Joan Upton Hall calls this writer's disease *be-verb-itis,* an overdependence on forms of the verb *to be.*

The sentence, *There was a foul odor in the room* could be written as *John smelled a foul odor in the room,* but I preferred a different approach based on my belief that when writing in limited viewpoint, it is seldom necessary to tell readers what the viewpoint character sees, smells, tastes, hears, or feels (through the sense of touch). My solution would be to pair the noun "odor" with an active verb, such as, *A foul odor filled the room.*

The book doctor wouldn't have objected to that wording, necessarily, but he acted like the proverbial duck pouncing on a June bug when I treated be-verb-itis by taking a heavier dose of medicine with a sentence like, *A foul odor assaulted John's nose.*

But his criticism reached a new level whenever I wrote a sentence that paired an abstraction with an active verb and a human object. If I remember correctly, the sentence *Regret tapped him on the shoulder,* which I have to admit I still kind of like, resulted in a lecture about the *pathetic fallacy* and *keeping agency with the human.*

The term pathetic fallacy is not pejorative in nature, but refers to the treatment of inanimate objects as if they had human feelings, thought, or sensations. These concepts are connected and deserve a chapter of their own (in a subsequent book in this series), but suffice it to say here that he convinced me of the error of my ways in trying to over-medicate be-verb-itis.

The third ailment and its remedy go to the heart of a mystery/thriller's story structure.

In Chapter Eight I quoted a rejection letter in which an agent said he wanted to see more forensic and investigative details as the sleuth solved the mystery. The revised manuscript I subsequently offered him for another look had been expanded with 120 pages of carefully researched technical accident investigation specifics. When the book doctor read this manuscript for the first time, he noted that these extra pages did not serve the story well, and he prescribed a treatment called the *budding flower approach.*

"Extraneous technical detail is the death of tension in a thriller. Your objective should be to have each piece of evidence lead to one of two results: a red herring *[a clue or piece of information which is intended to be misleading, or distracting from the actual issue]* or a crucial step toward solving the mystery. It's like the opening of a flower, but one petal at a time."

Unless a writer shuns outside input and remains in isolation, conflicting criticism, suggestions, and advice such as that offered by the agent and the book doctor are an unavoidable reality. Dealing with it takes experience, learning how to evaluate mutually exclusive inputs like, "Give me more of this," followed by "You have too much of this."

What's a writer to do?

In the end, the book doctor's approach won out, and I continued with yet another revision for the specific purpose of adding some attitude to the characters in *Pilot Error*, reducing my tendency to be fallaciously pathetic, and creating a flower with petals that open individually.

Thirteen-The Zoom Lens

What is psychic distance and how do I manipulate it?
Smile, viewpoint character, you're on candid camera.

Notable events in our lives occur separately or simultaneously by pure chance, calculated design, destiny, or a combination of the three based on a person's core belief system. As relates to my writer's journey, the next milestone appeared out of the ether.

In Chapter Five I mentioned joining the Novel-In-Progress Group of Austin, and I had been a regular participant for a number of years when a member of that group invited me to join an offshoot that met weekly rather than semi-monthly. With fewer members, more frequent meetings, shorter submissions, and the opportunity to submit every week for a steady flow of input, I accepted and began submitting from *Red Line,* the sequel to *Pilot Error.*

I had about half the novel written in first draft. Submitting about ten pages per week provided feedback in small chunks that were relatively easy to consider and implement. With the concept of total characterization so recently explored, I addressed it as one of my focal points and began receiving positive responses from reviewers on the improvements they noted.

A member of that group provided the next addition to my writer's toolkit, John Gardner's concept of "psychic distance." It came to me at a meeting in the form of five sentences to illustrate the psychic-distance continuum from what Gardner called vast at one end to nil at the other. It would be melodramatic to refer to this as a jaw-dropping moment, but that's the way it felt. From Gardner's *The Art of Fiction:*

1. It was winter of the year 1853. A large man stepped out of a doorway.
2. Henry J. Warburton had never much cared for snowstorms.
3. Henry hated snowstorms.
4. God how he hated these damn snowstorms.
5. Snow. Under your collar, down inside your shoes, freezing and plugging up your miserable soul.

For an excellent third party description of psychic distance and how to use it, see Emma Darwin's post in her "This Itch of Writing" blog.

Without having yet read Gardner's original description or anyone else's interpretation, here's what I got out of it the first time I saw it: a large man, Henry J. Warburton, Henry, he, you. The subject in the first sentence holds the reader at a distance, and in the last pulls the reader within the subject's skin and even deeper.

The next time I sat down to both *Pilot Error* and *Red Line*, a combination of total characterization and psychic distance seemed to add a filter to the computer screen that highlighted text in various colors, as if to identify where attention to these concepts could improve the reader's connection to the viewpoint character.

As I began incorporating these concepts, another milestone in the journey appeared in the form of an online beta reader I met on a forum dedicated to writing and submitting query letters to agents. She had read a number of versions of my query and offered to look at some of the novel. I'd seen enough of her comments to trust her skill, and this would be the first time in a long while that a "cold" reader would review a portion of the manuscript.

There's a saying that even a blind hog can find an acorn, and in this case it was my good fortune to receive from this reader a single suggestion that helped accomplish two objectives simultaneously. I paraphrase:

"Although I read thrillers almost exclusively, I'm not a pilot and your technical detail can create a problem when I don't understand something as well as I might like. I don't know if it's going to be important to the story, so I'm tempted to stop reading and do some research just in case. You can really help your readers keep up by recognizing these places and reversing the character's camera from focusing outward to inward. Let us experience in plain language the viewpoint character's interpretation of what's going on.

"That serves another important function, to keep readers in tune with the main character's analysis and interpretation of the clues, even when he's wrong. We go along for the ride down the blind alley of false conclusions. And since we are seeing the story from the antagonist's viewpoint as well, we may know that this alley also contains danger, a great tension-builder."

In combination, the lessons learned during this revision of *Pilot Error* felt as if they were taking the story to a new level. I've always considered writing the best story I can as my primary objective. The problem with this philosophy, however, is that it creates a nebulous and unattainable goal when considering that the next revision might be better. And what about the one after that?

The practical answer to that dilemma is to alter the objective slightly, to write the best story I can *at my current level of craftsmanship*. Then the question becomes, "When is it good enough to compete?"

The time had come to find out.

Fourteen–The Query Wars

Mistake #1: Confusing a query letter with a synopsis.
Mistake #2: Writing a business-letter query rather than
an evocative one.
Mistake #3: Thinking that writing a novel qualifies you to
write about it.
Cutting to the chase with the key ingredients of a query
letter that worked.

With a heavily revised manuscript ready to submit to agents, I began researching the query business and discovered a brand-new world dominated by the Internet. Not only had the submission process changed, but agents were blogging a constant stream of advice about how to write good query letters. I spent the better part of two months compiling as many different source references as I could find and began drafting queries. The original query that had previously resulted in a request for a full manuscript became v1.0. I tried a new one and labeled it v2.0, and kept track of minor changes to that version by adding a .1, .2, etc.

Over the course of many months, I tried out different versions on anyone I could hogtie and force to read them. I also joined QueryTracker.net (QT), a website dedicated to writing and submitting effective queries. Among other tools, the Query Review forum allows you to post yours and receive feedback. It didn't take long to realize that just as in critique groups, the quality of review depends upon the reviewer, and certain screen names began to stand out as being worthy of close attention to the advice being offered.

From the beginning of the Query Wars, I faced the same dilemma as with the manuscript. How will I know when it's good enough?

The practical solution to answering this question became that of a simple test. Could I read the newest version a few days later and maintain the same level of satisfaction I had immediately after writing it? With that criterion as my standard, I reached v21.1 before deciding that it might be the one.

Before email submissions became more common than not, the standard submission package consisted of the query, a synopsis, and the first three chapters or fifty pages, whichever was less. The consensus among writers seemed to be that agents would look at the synopsis only after they had read the writing sample, and the purpose was to determine whether the writer had plotted the remainder of the story well enough to call it a novel. At that time, the desired synopsis length as expressed by agents varied between two and ten pages. I had written three versions, short, medium, and long, so I dusted off these versions and began reading the synopsis review section on QT.

It didn't take long to discover that the importance of the synopsis had apparently lessened in the years since I last submitted any material. Fewer agents required it as a part of the initial submission package, and although they might want one included with a partial or full manuscript, how well the synopsis was written didn't receive the same emphasis that it used to.

Unwilling to accept that assumption and be caught unprepared, I used previous versions to draft a five-page synopsis and posted it on QT. It received a number of views and a few comments. One forum member took the time to shorten it to about half its original length, and suggested that the synopsis should be written as if I were telling a friend about a movie I'd seen. Another said not to sweat it too much, keep it under two pages, tell the main plot points, don't mention any characters that don't play an important role in the outcome and be sure to reveal the ending. The consensus: most agents skim a synopsis to see if there is a real story with a solid resolution. Beyond that, they probably don't read it that closely.

At this point, I had a query letter that still read well after aging for a while, and a synopsis that met all the current criteria as documented on the QT website. The time had come to investigate the numerous tools offered there for managing submissions to agents, and what an eye-opening experience it was. Only a few years had passed since I last submitted, and the entire process had changed dramatically.

No longer do writers have to purchase books whose information can be outdated before it appears on the shelves, and then spend hours calling the agencies to confirm the accuracy of data crucial for the query letter. Agents speak to writers directly through websites, blogs, tweets, and who knows what's next? Third-party websites provide enormous amounts of easily accessible information. Forums allow writers to share experiences, knowledge and specific expertise, and to offer each other mutual support through the often agonizing process of trying to obtain representation.

One of the problems created by this easy access is deciding when you have enough information to conclude that you don't need any more. I'm particularly vulnerable to the pitfalls of never-ending preparation. Ask any of my writer friends and they will probably say something to the effect of, "How many drafts does it take? He's revised that novel at least thirteen times, written over forty query letters, and just finished the eighth version of the synopsis. When is he going to *submit* something?"

And that was an accurate observation. Some fellow writers even predicted that I'd never get past the preparation stage. But I set out to prove them wrong and developed an agent list from the QT database, which includes over 1000 agents. I refined the search criteria by selecting mystery, thriller, and suspense genres and restricted the search to only those agents who accepted unsolicited queries. That produced an alphabetical list of about 160.

Additional sorting criteria provide tools for customizing the list using four columns with information as reported by QT members: total number of queries submitted to each agent, number of rejections, number of requests for additional material, percentage of rejections, and percentage of requests for additional materials. Clicking on the top of a column ranks the agents in descending order according to that parameter.

Sorted by total number of submissions, for example, the list indicates agent popularity with QT members. To sort by percentage of requests ranks agents according to the historical likelihood that they responded favorably to queries. I chose that criterion because it seemed the most helpful in determining which agents were more likely to be receptive to unpublished authors. The next task was to assimilate all the information provided for each agent.

Beginning at the top, I visited the agency/agent websites for biographical information, preferences, submission guidelines, client lists, and comments from QT members about each agent. It didn't take long to become overwhelmed by all the particulars, and I decided to complete this initial scouting process before sending out any queries.

My original objective was to evaluate specific details for each agent and come up with a ranking of my own, but that didn't work. With the exception of a few agents who appeared on paper to be especially well matched with my novel, I concluded that trying to cherry-pick an agent was futile. They'd either pick me or they wouldn't, and predicting that was like trying to nail Jell-O to the ceiling.

A friend and fellow writer tells a query-war story about an agent he picked as a long shot. She responded with a request for additional material and said something to the effect of, "A main character who burns down his own house. I love it!" She declined to offer representation, but the moral of the story was clear to me: query widely, because you never know what might pique the agent's interest.

Following a period of sustained data collection and analysis, my self-image as a take-charge kind of guy needed alteration when I found myself avoiding the QT bookmark in my browser. One click and I'd be back on the front lines, but for a few months I avoided doing that. My procrastination was caused by lingering uncertainty about the quality of the query letter and writing sample that constitute the meat of a submission package.

If the query letter doesn't do its job, the agent will never read the sample and will auto-reject with a typical "Dear Author" form reply that strikes both the novice and the experienced query warrior directly in the heart with a steel spike.

And the worst part, if there can be such a thing, is that you have no way of finding out where in the package the agent quit reading. Few if any agents at this stage of the writer-agent interaction will spend even a second explaining their reason(s) for rejecting you. Blind querying is terribly frustrating.

This roadblock on the highway to publication cannot be eliminated until a very significant event occurs: you receive a request for either a partial or a full manuscript. The moment that happens, even if it's only your first request and it represents the interest of only one agent, you know that you have an initial package with the potential to open the gateway to publication a little bit further.

That's a tremendous confidence builder. It's also very dangerous to a writer's psyche if you allow it to fill your head with the fantasy that this is equivalent to obtaining representation by the agent. The road ahead is still very steep, and it's not an easy climb.

Query Letter 101 from the notes of Tosh McIntosh:

The objective: use the most commonly recommended structure as a template for building a query letter that works. The method: identify the specific elements from the first 20-40 pages of the novel that belong in the query, and highlight the personal experience that uniquely qualifies the author to write the story.

From the agents:

- Start with the story rather than title, word count, genre.
- Use short, declarative sentences.
- The short-form query demands simple structures.
- Your objective: compel the agent to read the first five pages.
- Rhetorical questions don't work.
- Start with the hero.
- Who is the main character?
- What choice (conflict) does he face?

- What are the consequences of making/not making the choice?
- What's amiss here, and what's going to happen because of it?
- Use these to structure the query and do not try to tell the whole story.
- Avoid reporter mode: standing back and observing.
- Get into the story and be partisan, subjective.
- Make us see what life is like for the hero and why we should care.

A successful format of sentences:
- Provide the setup.
- Introduce the antagonist.
- Set up the initial conflict.
- Increase the threat.
- Make it even worse.
- Illustrate the stakes.

With hours of research as my guide, I developed a shopping list of suitable query material from my novel.

Who is the MC? Provide an answer that spurs interest, an insight that makes him unique, an attention grabber.
- Lost his father to an accident caused by pilot error.
- Became a pilot and an accident investigator.
- Fears that the sins of the father will be visited upon the son and he'll make a fatal mistake.
- Career objective: do all he can to prevent any son from losing a dad to pilot error.
- Unwavering dedication to the investigative process, te-

nacious, persistent, never give up.

- Ultimate career goal: advance to Chief of the Aviation Division of NTSB, because from that position he can most effectively fulfill his career objective.
- Considers himself a dedicated husband and father.
- But he's wrong about that and his family has gotten less of him than his career.
- Suspicious of all politicians, believes that absolute power leads to inevitable corruption and abuse.
- Honors the military and their sacrifice, but not how they are used by politicians.
- Believes in the rule of law and that America shouldn't descend to the tactics of its enemies.
- Is well informed of the current controversy over possible government-sanctioned illegal tactics in the war on terror and of the victim's threat not to go down alone.
- Believes that if the victim did violate the law by doing what he was asked to do, he's a loyal patriot rather than a criminal.
- For the President to make the victim a scapegoat is just another example of abusing power.

Plot catalyst/inciting event: What is the choice the MC has to make, the conflict he faces?

- Victim's death is far too convenient not to cause suspicion that the airplane might have been sabotaged to silence him and protect the President.
- Victim's reputation as an aviator without the skills to be flying a private jet single-pilot is a perfect setup for sabotage designed to lead investigators to the conclusion of pilot error.
- The sabotage has to be well disguised and hard to find.

- To replace the MC with a protégé of the character's boss is extra protection against discovery and consistent with a cover-up.
- The MC has planned for a backup team leader in case the next investigation overlaps important family milestone events.
- The MC's father-self urges him to stay at home.
- His investigator-self urges him to resist being removed and to lead the investigation.

Consequences: What will happen if the MC does/does not make the choice?

- To stay at home turns a blind eye to the possibility that a man has been murdered and justice will not be given a chance.
- To lead the investigation with a private agenda of searching for evidence of murder violates his duty to the NTSB.
- This career/family tug-of-war is tipped in favor of career by the MC's firm belief in two things: 1) if he doesn't lead the investigation, evidence of sabotage will never be found, and 2) regardless of position, no one should get away with murder.
- This decision sets the MC on a collision course with the cover-up being run by the President's most trusted advisor and his minion, a hired assassin.

The MC's story arc:

- He's a family man/accident investigator, period.
- When he forces himself back onto the investigation and thwarts the attempt to remove him, he does so for reasons that John Truby calls an "immoral act." The

MC has assumed the unofficial role of murder investigator.

- It's immoral because it violates his charter from the NTSB: determine the cause of accidents with the sole purpose of enhancing flight safety.
- It violates his charter because he takes with him to Colorado a hidden agenda: find the sabotage he believes exists. Under no circumstances are NTSB employees to investigate criminal wrongdoing.
- He's playing a role now, acting as if nothing's unusual while he hides his true intentions.
- When he reluctantly has to admit that all evidence points to pilot error, and the inconsistencies he finds in no way meet the litmus test for calling in the FBI, he commits another immoral act by sharing this information with a reporter.
- That collaboration produces another piece of inconsistent evidence, the meaning of which he cannot surmise, unless . . .
- He commits his third immoral act by tampering with existing evidence.
- By committing his own pilot error that nearly kills him, he *proves* sabotage . . . but only to himself and the reporter because they've lost control of the evidence.
- He commits a fourth immoral act by sharing everything on-the-record with the reporter for the specific purpose of bringing the conspirators into the open.
- It works, puts a number of people at risk and results in three more deaths.
- Now it's really personal, and the MC makes the final transition into righteous avenger.

Author bio: Why I'm the only person who can write this

novel.

- Retired USAF Lt. Colonel with over twenty years active-duty service as a fighter pilot
- Two combat tours in Vietnam flying the F-4 Phantom.
- Operations Officer and instructor at the USAF Fighter Weapons School (Air Force version of the Navy's Top Gun)
- Air Force expert on the laser target designator system that preceded the smart bomb systems used in both Gulf wars
- Ten years as a commercial airline pilot
- Ten years as a corporate jet pilot
- Current owner/pilot of two sport airplanes.

The query letter that produced results:

Dear Agent:

In twenty years as a crash investigator, Nick Phillips has discovered evidence of fatal pilot error often enough to expect it. So when a private jet slams into a ridgeline, he anticipates finding one more example of preventable death. But only until a far more disturbing possibility emerges.

The victim faced indictment for war crimes as the leader of an anti-terror assassination squad. What if he signed his own death warrant with very public threats to implicate the high-level government officials who sanctioned his targets?

Nick focuses on the victim's most obvious vulnerability, a lethal combination of mediocre pilot skills and a giant ego. His frequent solo flights to a Colorado mountain airport at night and in any weather conditions could have offered someone a perfect opportunity to conceal airborne murder behind the smokescreen of pilot error.

To prove his theory, Nick scrutinizes the wreckage for indications of sabotage. When he finds nothing, and the preponderance of evidence points directly to pilot error, he's left with only one lead. Someone visited the crash site before first responders arrived. Who was it, what did they do, and why?

Nick's tenacious search for answers ultimately results in four additional deaths and puts him in the crosshairs of a special ops assassin. From a wilderness gun battle, to a narrow escape after burglarizing the killer's Florida mansion, to a dogfight in the Colorado skies, Nick follows a trail of conspiracy all the way into the Oval Office.

I am a retired USAF Lt. Colonel with four decades in tactical fighters, commercial airliners and corporate jets. *Pilot Error* is a 100,000-word aviation mystery that blends the accuracy of personal experience with in-depth technical knowledge of crash investigation. Readers will tighten their seatbelts as Nick Phillips unravels the twisted threads of sabotage and murder.

FIFTEEN-ABNA

What's in a contest?
Follow the rules . . . exactly.
Keep the lid on the expectation jar.
The overnight rule and why it's important.
Contests and querying agents have more in
common than not.
Consider any contest as a learning opportunity.
Disclaimer: This chapter presents my personal
experience with only one contest.

I love acronyms. Especially pronounceable ones. My fondness probably began when I entered the military, and especially because I became an aviator.

Those of us who fly use discipline-specific acronyms as convenient shorthand to streamline communication. But pilots have another objective, which is to confuse any non-flyers who might happen to overhear our conversations. That lends a degree of mystery to what we do. It's all a smokescreen, of course. Almost anyone can learn to fly an airplane, but we'd prefer keeping that to ourselves.

The title of this chapter refers to the *Amazon Breakthrough Novel Award*. A friend and fellow writer mentioned the contest, or I wouldn't have known about it. He'd entered the previous year and advanced to the quarter-finals. Considering the contest accepts up to 5000 entries, that's quite an achievement.

One really cool benefit was the gift of a manuscript critique by none other than *Publisher's Weekly*. He told me that the comments he received really helped him see areas in the novel that could be improved.

I mentioned in the previous chapter that I had the novel *Pilot Error* ready to begin submitting to agents with a query letter, writing sample, and synopsis. And although this was without question the best package I'd ever assembled, it still didn't engender the final bit of confidence I sought to overcome my apprehension about wasting the opportunity to query any of the 160 agents on my list. That seems like a lot until the rejections start pouring in.

As it turned out, entering the contest became another significant milestone in my writer's journey.

The rules specified that entries must consist of three items: a pitch (300-word maximum), an excerpt (3000-5000 words), and the complete manuscript (50,000-150,000 words).

Round one involved only the pitch, which meant I had 300 words or less to convince a judge that my novel deserved to be advanced to round two where the excerpt would be read. The pitch, therefore, effectively served the same function as a query letter to an agent.

And while the judges were Amazon editors and not literary agents, I couldn't pass up the opportunity to use the contest as a testing ground for my query letter. Both had the same job to do: engage a reader's interest enough to want to read more.

That conclusion assumed, of course, that guidelines for writing the pitch were similar to those for a query letter. Here's what the contest information said about the pitch:

> *A cover letter or "pitch" which explains your nov-*
> *el's concept is required. This must be 300 words or less.*
> *The Pitch is more than just a summary; it needs to be a*
> *well-written explanation of what the book is about. Talk*
> *about your novel's strengths with respect to how it is being*
> *evaluated. Think about the elements chosen on which to*
> *judge your novel for the purpose of this contest: its overall*
> *strength, plot development, character development, origi-*
> *nality of idea, and writing style or prose. Take the time to*
> *study your intended market and make sure your Pitch dem-*
> *onstrates that you understand how your book fits within*
> *this market and how it will identify with your audience.*
> *Remember, the book should resonate with who your read-*
> *ers are. The Pitch should be a concise explanation of your*
> *book and why the reader would want to read your novel.*

This description presented a problem, because it suggested what query letter guidelines referred to as the business letter approach, further labeled as always appropriate. But in reading sample query letters used by agents to share what works, I had noted that many of them didn't talk about the novel, but about the story in a concise, clear narrative that reflects the tone of the work and the voice of the author. I had embraced this evocative approach as the one for me.

On the ABNA forum, however, members were actively engaged in discussing the pitch, and I found some thread comments that sounded pretty good to me. Here's one:

> *The only things you need to know are that your pitch*
> *must be three hundred words or less, or it will not load. If*
> *your pitch sucks, it will be rejected. The rest are details. Do*

not worry about following every rule. There are no rules to writing. There are no rules to pitch writing. Be brilliant or die. That's it. Why should I spend twenty bucks to buy your book? Sell me. There are however, guidelines. Do mention your genre, and put your novel title in all caps. Do make your pitch interesting. Do give a flavor to your story.

I realized that to ignore contest advice in favor of that posted on a forum might lead me astray, but there's a difference between what an official might think and how a writer approaches the problem of generating interest in a novel on the basis of 300 words or less. I'd already tried that with my query letter, so the question once again became, "Is it good enough?"

Most writers I know will tell you they would rather hit themselves in the thumb with a hammer than try to write a compelling, evocative blurb about their novel. How can something that looks so easy be so hard?

Walk into a bookstore and randomly consider any dust jacket description. It either captures your interest so you'll plop down the bucks and take it home, or it doesn't. The difference between the two probably has more to do with what the blurb says than how it says it. That's because there's a proven structural formula for success, certain key elements that create effective advertising.

One of the suggestions about how to write a pitch is to spend time reading a bunch of them. I've done that, ended up excited about trying it for my novel, sat down at the computer and stared at a blank screen for an hour before deciding to try again another day. What's up with that?

The only answer I've come up with is that it requires a different set of skills, and writing the novel didn't prepare me in advance for writing *about* it.

Excessive familiarity might have something to do with it. I'd spent so much time with the manuscript, enough to complete over 13 drafts as I struggled to improve both the story and my ability to tell it effectively. I'd nearly memorized every word, and to condense 100,000 of them into 300 or less was like slaughtering the other 97,700. Did I mention how hard that's been?

The good news is that the most common guidelines limit query letters to about 300 words and I had a polished one ready to go. The query also included required information unnecessary for the pitch, which provided the opportunity to remove it and add more of the good stuff. Beginning with the latest version of the query, I began revising it while keeping one eye glued to the word counter. After completing five different versions, I found myself halfway through a ten-rounder with a heavyweight. Anyone foolish enough to tackle the daunting challenge of writing a novel knows all about this phenomenon.

Throughout my struggles to create a query letter for agents and the pitch for the contest, I used the overnight rule, which meant that I kept revising and tweaking and fiddling in search of that magical moment in which I opened the document in the morning and could honestly say, "I don't think I can do better than this right now." It's like a warm fuzzy that spreads over me, along with a smile, a nod, and the confidence that the words serve the intended purpose.

The problem is the rarity of the occurrence. You expect to read the final version and it sucks. A conversation with your muse ensues. (Pardon me for the rhyme, but I couldn't help myself.)

"Who wrote this garbage?" you ask.

"You did," the muse answers.

"I did not."

"Yes, you did. If you don't like it, get back to work."

There may be writers who can accomplish that quickly. I envy them. For the rest of us, we try to help each other as best we can. So I called in reinforcements by asking a few writer buddies for their opinions. We're all aware of the hazards in doing that and the adage, "Don't ask the question if you can't stand the answer." But we understand that the recipient is free to accept or reject the suggestions and no one allows feelings to get in the way of respectful interaction. As always, that helped a lot.

Rather than revising the same query multiple times, one of my writer friends prefers to start each new version from scratch. I decided to try that and began with a blank document. The result morphed over the next two days into something that worked well. Or at least I thought it did, until that version began to stink. Garbage-dump-quality stink.

In frustration, or maybe desperation, I opened up the previous version, and although to call it an epiphany might be overstating the case, a couple of small tweaks and moving sentences around in one paragraph resulted in a kind of "Ohmigosh" reaction.

After multiple overnight suck-test gestation periods, a few minor tweaks, and the addition of three words (for a total of 300), I was finally able to call the ABNA pitch a wrap. I uploaded it along with the excerpt and the complete manuscript, then returned to the business of submitting to agents. Which was a good thing, because it kept my mind from wandering to the contest and engaging in wishful thinking.

Sixteen-A Dichotomy Of Opinion

After you enter a contest, follow Uncle Vinnie's advice
and "Fuget abaht it."
A request for a full means only that your query letter and
writing sample worked.
Expect contrary evaluations. They are the nature
of the beast.
Ultimately, yours is the only voice with any authority.
Listen to it and believe.

With nothing more to do for the ABNA contest except wait for the results of Round One, I returned to the Query Wars and began fine-tuning my list of agents in preparation for submitting once again. And when advancement to Round Two validated the effectiveness of my pitch, the time had come for a full-scale assault on the gatekeepers of legacy publishing.

I used the pitch to hone the query letter one last time and combined it with a writing sample identical to the opening of the longer contest excerpt. In short order I received requests for two full manuscripts and two partials, one of which resulted in a further request for a full. This was an exciting time in my writer's journey as I awaited the results of Round Two.

It's easy to compare my reactions to requests from agents with that of learning that I had not advanced to the contest quarter-finals. They don't exist in the same emotional universe. I'm talking light-years of separation.

In trying to make sense of the dichotomy, all I knew was that four agents had reacted favorably and two Amazon reviewers in combination had not rated my excerpt within the top 25%. It didn't take much more than that to consider the reviewers' opinions suspect.

Reviewers for the contest are called "Vine Voices," readers who have reached an elevated status with Amazon through an established history of writing reviews. Vine Voices remain anonymous, so there's no way for a contestant to check their qualifications for reviewing any particular type of novel. The total number of excerpts and the Vine Voices available to review them introduce a significant element of luck into the process, especially when considering that every fiction genre except young adult is included in one of the two submission categories. With no practical way to match a Vine Voice with an excerpt from the Vine Voice's preferred genres, mismatches are bound to occur. At least in part, I think that's what happened in my case.

While both reviewers thought the opening did a good job of introducing more questions than providing answers (which I assume is their way of saying that's what a mystery should do), the negative comments included imagery that didn't work well and clunky writing. It should come as no surprise that I don't agree with those assessments of my excerpt, but their opinions are what count in the contest. I knew that when I entered, so any complaints are nothing more than sour grapes.

But I couldn't help trying to assess the review quality of the following comment: "There wasn't much dialogue, and it's difficult to evaluate a novel without seeing more of it."

I thought their job was to judge the excerpt, not the novel. But beyond that, this is a mystery/thriller, and a very common opening structure is to show initial events from the viewpoint of a bad guy and a victim before the main character arrives on scene.

In the first two chapters of my novel, one character is on a clandestine mission of nefarious intent and trying very hard not to be seen by anyone, much less have a conversation. The other character is flying an airplane by himself in bad weather and trying to land at a mountain airport at night, and he speaks only periodically to an air traffic controller.

Apparently, it's the novel structure the reviewer didn't care for, and the resulting scarcity of dialogue became a more important criterion than the quality of it.

And what about this comment? "The author needs to reduce the numbers in the flight scene."

One of this novel's primary objectives is to put readers in the pilot's seat, around which there are lots of numbers. Other readers have told me I do a good job of presenting technical data in the right proportion with plain language so that the flying scenes don't read as if they are intended only for aviators. Apparently this reviewer didn't agree, and I'd bet there aren't any techno-thrillers on his or her bookshelf.

Okay, I can consider both of these comments as the result of pure chance. The contest offered only two categories, one devoted entirely to young adult novels, and the second to everything else, which represents a very large amount of diversity. I have no idea whether Amazon attempted to match up reviewers with genres, and I can't imagine that individual reviewers were equally knowledgeable and proficient at evaluating them all. Such is the writer's life and there's nothing I can do about that. The next comment, however, is a different beast altogether.

"The author didn't provide any connection between the two characters, and that was confusing."

Really? I have to say that I am baffled by this criticism. To explain why, all I ask is that you trust me when I submit that what follows is an accurate narrative picture of the opening to *Pilot Error*.

At 2:47 a.m., a man named Wilson, armed with a suppressed pistol, climbs an airport perimeter fence, sneaks past a security guard he doesn't want to kill, and picks the lock on a door of a hangar belonging to **Schiller Aviation.** Once inside, he plants a padded mailer from a **navigation chart provider** and addressed to **Larchmont** Enterprises, LLC, in a box labeled **N924DP**, the discrete, unique registration number of an airplane. After a near run-in with the guard, the man leaves without being detected and rushes off to a "rendezvous with someone else's death."

In the next chapter, a man named **Larchmont** is in a bulletproof Lincoln Town Car with a driver and a bodyguard carrying an assault rifle. Readers learn in a short flashback why he's being so careful, to the point of having a bomb-sniffing dog check out his private jet before takeoff. While waiting at **Schiller Aviation**, Larchmont sees a news report that proves he is the last man standing outside the White House who knows the details of a clandestine operation that if made public could bring down the President. It's time to run for his life. At the jet, readers see an envelope from a **navigation chart provider**. Once Larchmont is airborne, they hear him using the call sign **N924DP**.

Okay, here's my assessment. This novel is an aviation mystery. Mysteries have clues. It's my job to play fair with readers and provide clues that aren't so cryptic that readers have no chance to think, "Oh, now that's important." I think the opening pages more than adequately provide a connection between Chapters One and Two. If you agree with me, then consider this.

Contest entrants have to accept the role of chance in how their excerpts are assigned to Vine Voice Reviewers. They also have to accept that reviewers are vetted by Amazon well enough to provide a reasonably fair evaluation of the excerpts. But what I think stretches the limit of acceptance is for a reviewer apparently to need footnotes to keep up with what's going on. To contend that there's no connection between the first two characters in my novel is, frankly, bogus.

They're called clues for a reason. Readers of mysteries look for clues, and trying to solve the mystery before the sleuth does is a major component of their widespread popularity.

End of whine-a-thon.

Walking away from the disappointing contest results was relatively easy. At that moment I had a 43% request rate from agents for additional material, and the opinion of two Vine Voice Reviewers didn't mean much.

Over the next few months I continued to query agents while waiting for verdicts from my three fulls and one partial. Unfortunately, my initial success didn't repeat, and one by one, three of the four agents with manuscripts passed on the opportunity.

Not too long ago, a writer could count on two things when dealing with agents.

First, rejection letters received as a result of an initial query and writing sample were form-letter generic and told you nothing useful, like answering the question, "When did you quit reading and click on *Auto Reject*?" As much as that frustrates a writer not to know whether the problem is with the query letter, the writing sample, or both, it's fully understandable. Agents aren't in the business of critiquing submission packages.

Second, rejection letters from partial or full manuscript submissions were usually personalized at least to the point of indentifying specific reasons that you could evaluate and decide whether they were worth addressing before sending out more queries. It's like coming home from an unsuccessful job interview in which you smiled a lot only to discover that the spinach salad you had for lunch left a remnant lodged between a pearly white lateral incisor and a canine. You don't *really* know, do you?

Today, only the first of those things is still true. And so, after receiving obviously generic rejections to one partial and two full manuscripts, I waited without much optimism for a decision from the agent with the remaining full.

In the vernacular, it's called a nudge: a short, follow-up query to ask politely, "Whassup with my novel?" The agent insisted that she remained interested and asked for patience. But by the time I had waited another month, my forbearance tank registered empty. I sounded retreat from the battlefields of the Query Wars by removing my novel from consideration. Unlike earlier query campaigns, however, this one left me with a viable alternative.

Some writers, especially those who have successfully passed through the agent gatekeepers into the world of traditional publishing, consider any other road as the pathway of quitters, wannabe writers who flood the market with stories unfit to be considered by the reading public.

I understand the sentiment and wholeheartedly agree that today's streamlined process of publishing a novel in eBook and print-on-demand formats has tempted many writers to bypass the essential steps of learning the craft.

That said, the further conclusion that all legacy-published novels are worth reading and no indie-published novels deserve a moment of our time is nonsense.

In anticipation of not being offered representation by an agent, early in the query wars I began planning for the day when it would be up to me to make it happen.

In Book Two of *Wings On My Words,* tales from the writer's desk will continue with the aftermath of the decision to Go Indie!

# # #

PREVIEW OF

PILOT ERROR

a novel by

TOSH McINTOSH

CHAPTER ONE

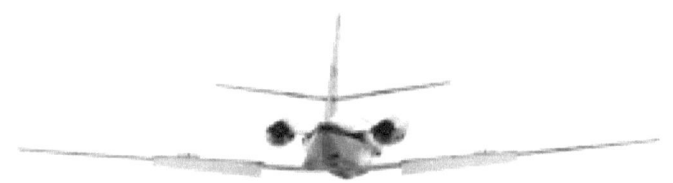

Wilson didn't *want* to kill the guard and leave a mess behind. Someone might get curious, nose around, ask questions. No, the job tonight required stealth. He loved that word. And the synonyms, like furtiveness. That just sounded right, especially when whispered. It slid off the tongue. He'd prolong the "s" and think of himself as a viper in the night, coiled like a spring, silent and deadly.

From his hiding place near the edge of the dark, woody greenbelt, he peered through the airport perimeter chain-link fence at the hangar thirty yards away. Raindrops slapped on the hood of his parka and the blanket of leaves around him. Cold wind rustled the branches above his head. He preferred working with nature's white noise as an ally, but tonight it favored the guard, all the more reason for caution.

Wilson had initially accepted this assignment on contingency because he'd never tried to penetrate the secure area of an airport. Especially after 9/11, it seemed far too risky. But his concern proved to be groundless. Of the 19,000 airports in the US, only a small percentage received the security upgrades designed to prevent aircraft from being used as weapons of terror, and for good reason. To fly the largest airplane based here into a skyscraper would be like a suicidal bug smashing into the windshield of a Mack truck.

Earlier that day, he had masqueraded as a salesman for an alarm company and offered the owner of the hangar a security survey. The man laughed him out of the office. Said he couldn't afford it, especially to prevent something that had never happened. Besides, the airport authority paid for a night watchman. Didn't cost him a penny. Now, Wilson understood why.

The guard, a typical rent-a-cop "door rattler," sang country music while walking his rounds. The fool announced he was coming. And he never varied his routine. Every half-hour since midnight, he'd taken a smoke break, protected from the steady drizzle by the awning over a door on the back side of the hangar. Atomic-clock predictable.

Wilson peeled back the cuff of his parka and glanced at his watch: 2:47. The guard was taking his nicotine hit fifteen minutes early. Wilson needed less than ten minutes and could still do this without bloodshed unless the idiot started chain-smoking.

He pulled the pistol from his waistband through an opening in the outer pocket liner of his parka and screwed the silencer into the barrel. Then he checked for a round in the chamber and a full magazine, and slipped the weapon in his parka's belt. Eyes on the guard, he waited.

Two minutes later, the guard dropped the butt on the ramp, ground it out with his boot and began walking toward the far end of the hangar. Wilson stepped up to the fence, reached above his head and shoved his fingers through the links. Lucky for him, it had no topping of razor wire and served primarily to keep deer off the runway. Just like his airport at home. He'd seen what colliding with a full-grown Bambi could do to an airplane on takeoff or landing, and it wasn't pretty.

As the guard turned the corner, Wilson climbed over the fence, ran across the ramp, unlocked the door with a battery-powered pick gun and stepped inside. A row of ceiling lights bathed the cavernous interior in ghostly white. Airplanes, portable worktables, and wheeled tool boxes were jammed together like a jigsaw puzzle. Faint odors of aviation maintenance lingered: fuel, oil, paint, heavy-duty cleaning chemicals. Comforting, in a way. Reminded him of his hangar.

Weaving through the maze, he made his way to a cabinet mounted on the opposite wall. Aircraft tail numbers identified the open, partitioned sections in the cabinet as distribution boxes for each of the airplanes based at Schiller Aviation. The section labeled N924DP held two tattered cardboard containers sitting side by side on a shelf.

He removed the one marked IN, knelt, and placed it on the concrete floor. In the beam of a small flashlight held in a nylon pouch sewn on his watch cap, he thumbed through the contents: two eight-by-ten-inch envelopes imprinted with the logo of a navigation chart provider and addressed to Larchmont Enterprises, LLC, one business envelope from the Golden Aircraft Company, and a small electrical part in a plastic baggie with a green SERVICEABLE tag. The innocuous, everyday items of aviation on their way to an airplane.

And inside his parka, an addition. He lifted out a padded mailing envelope and took one final look at the postage, address, and return labels. No one would ever guess it hadn't gone through the US mail. He placed the mailer in the container, returned it to the shelf and retraced his route across the hangar.

With his face close to the glass, he peered through the small window set into the door. No sign of the guard. Wilson eased the door open and looked to his left where the guard had always appeared from around the corner of the hangar, then to the right. Nothing. He took one step outside and froze.

Embedded within the sounds of rain and wind, something foreign drifted on the gusts. He closed his eyes and tuned out the background. After a few seconds, he retreated into the hangar and let the door close gently. Way early, the karaoke guard had suddenly turned even more unpredictable. Wilson pulled out the pistol, heavy in his hand, comforting. Like an addiction. The anticipation ratcheted up his heart rate just enough to heighten his senses and add another layer of *alert*. He sidestepped left past the hinge edge of the door.

After a moment the guard appeared in the window and stopped under the awning, two feet from the door and facing the forest. Wilson leaned to his right, took a quick peek down, noted the guard's duty belt with a radio and a flashlight carrier. No weapon. He relaxed a bit. All he had to do was wait a few minutes, watch the door handle for any movement to warn him—*damn it!* The door rested against the latch bolt and hadn't closed all the way. If the guy turned around and saw that . . .

Wilson flattened himself against the hangar wall, raised the pistol to the level of the guard's head and took up the tiny bit of slack in the double-action trigger. One step inside, he'd have to put the guy down. So much for an easy in and out.

After a few seconds, barely audible over the wind and rain, a click, a rasping snap, pause, another click. A Zippo lighter. Cigarette smoke drifted through the slim crack between the door and jamb. Wilson eased his pressure on the trigger and took a deep breath. The smoke awakened a familiar hunger that had never really left him.

He had quit over twenty years ago. For his health, although fear of cancer had nothing to do with it. On that night, two steps from the mark, Wilson's knife poised to strike home, the guy had ducked, swiveled, come in low, hard, and fast. Wilson had almost died, and the man's last words remained with him still: *I smelled you.*

He enjoyed a second-hand smoke until a boot wet-grated on concrete, stubbing out the cigarette. The guard began singing a recent country hit, something about being unlucky in love. Not bad, actually. He ought to turn in his flashlight for a microphone. The voice faded away as the guard continued his rounds.

Wilson lowered the pistol, breathed in deep, held it and let his pulse calm down a bit.

Over the years, in spite of all the planning and preparation for countless jobs, it so often came down to something as simple as this. One small coincidence either passes into history as a freebie or changes the complexion of future events. Tonight, he gladly accepted the gift.

Wilson opened the door and checked both ways. He slipped the pistol in a jacket pocket, stepped out, closed the door, and sprinted for the fence. Ten minutes in the greenbelt at a fast walk put him at the edge of the woods along a deserted street. On the other side in a motel parking lot sat his rental car, inconspicuous among many. Just the way he liked it. He closed his eyes to listen and zone in on the night. Nothing. He strode to the car and climbed in.

With the heater on high, he poured a cup of coffee from a thermos, wrapped his hands around the cup, and after a moment drained it in a few swallows. He shook the empty thermos, wishing for more. It felt like he'd never warm up. *Getting too old for this field stuff.*

He yanked off his gloves and blew into his hands, then took a small piece of notepaper from an outer pocket on his cargo pants and set it between his legs on the seat. He removed the flashlight from the pouch on his watch cap, held it close to the paper to shield it and focused the beam.

Holding his cell phone in the other hand, he entered the ten-digit sequence with his thumb, pausing after each number to concentrate before pressing the next one. When the complete phone number was displayed, he carefully compared each digit on the paper with the screen before he pressed TALK. After three rings and a beep, he said to the silence, "Operator Forty-One, activate, one hour," and turned off the phone.

So much for the groundwork. The time had come to watch and wait, to be there just in case. The anonymous voice would soon begin calling on the secure line, pestering Wilson about when it would happen. He would ignore the inquiries as he always did. Contact with clients occurred at his convenience. The next time they spoke, the topic would be money. Lots of it. Enough to call it quits.

And he was so ready. Ready to abandon the double life. Ready to live in the light. And maybe one day he'd be able to stop looking over his shoulder. No more nightmares with the eyes of the dead staring at him. Put his head on a pillow and leave it all behind for longer than a few hours.

A check in the rearview, both side mirrors, and all around the parking lot found nothing but dark rooms, sleeping cars, wet asphalt, and pale shafts of rain under yellow streetlights. He pulled the pistol out of his jacket and laid it in the seat by his leg, then eased the car out of the lot and accelerated into the night toward a rendezvous with someone else's death.

CHAPTER TWO

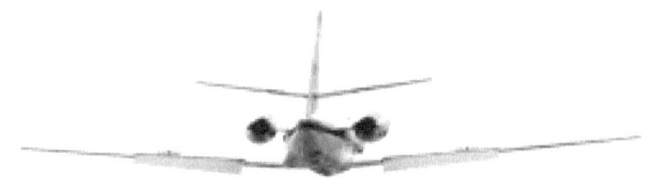

iles Larchmont stared into the early morning gloom through the rain-streaked, bulletproof left rear window of the Lincoln Town Car. He yawned, stretched and glanced at his watch. A long day awaited and he was already tired.

The dreary weather reminded him of that moment earlier in the year when he'd been partying for hours and the usual rabble of unrelenting paparazzi ambushed him coming out of a nightclub. Microphones jabbed at his face, bright camera lights blinded him, and a rapid-fire barrage of questions assaulted his eardrums. As his drinking buddies escorted him toward the car, two shouted queries cut through the fog of alcohol.

"What will you say to the American people?"

"Who do you think you are—?"

"A patriot, goddamn it!" His answer stilled the group in a freeze-frame of anticipation. Raindrops pattered on a forest of umbrellas. "Just what this country needs more than ever."

A companion gripped Larchmont's arm and turned him away.

Then, the life-altering question: "How about a real statement for a change?"

Yanking his arm free, he swiveled to face the bastards. "Tell them I won't be going down alone."

Two friends hustled him to the waiting limousine. He slumped in the rear seat along with the bitter knowledge that his loud mouth had done it once again. He'd give almost anything to rewind the tape and—

"We're here, Mr. Larchmont," said the driver.

Larchmont shook his head, sighed, and glanced out the windshield. A sign with the Schiller Aviation logo appeared in the headlight beams. The bodyguard riding shotgun lifted an assault rifle off the floor and nestled it in his lap as the driver pulled into a parking spot by the front entrance.

Larchmont opened his own door, climbed out onto the wet asphalt and looked up. Ragged clouds of the first autumn cold front skimmed overhead, glowing red from the hazard beacon atop the water tower adjacent to the hangar. Depressing. A perfect match to his mood. He faced the two men. "Take a close look at the jet. You got the dog coming?"

"Yes, sir," said the bodyguard. "That's the K-nine unit."

A dark van with no markings careened into the lot and skidded to a stop. A man in black fatigues hopped out and opened the sliding side door. Eager to sniff something, or maybe bite it, a German shepherd lurched against a heavy leash tied to a seat support.

Larchmont stayed behind the open door of the Town Car until the handler had the dog under control, then slammed the door and walked toward the main entrance. To the driver, he said, "Get to it. I'm in a hurry." He hadn't gone three steps when behind him, the rumble of a massive V8 announced the arrival of P. J. Knowles, Larchmont's personal mechanic.

Larchmont glanced over his shoulder. A black 1971 Pontiac GTO turned into the lot. Beads of rain covered the muscle car in glistening droplets on countless layers of wax, vivid evidence of the meticulous attention P.J. paid both to his car and to Larchmont's twin-engine jet.

P.J. revved the engine. Racing slicks spun on the asphalt in a spray of water. Larchmont waved hello, shook his head and continued toward the entrance. With 500 horsepower at his command, P.J. had a reputation as a wild child, especially on the open road. Larchmont shared the common opinion that the hot-rodder was living on borrowed time.

"Mr. Larchmont?"

Larchmont paused at the door and turned. "Morning, P.J."

P.J. trotted up, opened the door and motioned Larchmont through. "Are you flying today, sir? I didn't know."

"Not to worry. The jet's always ready to go, right?"

P.J.'s face registered instant displeasure at such an insulting question. "Absolutely, sir."

Larchmont always enjoyed needling his mechanic. Not a lot, his life was in the guy's hands, but just enough to keep him on his toes, paying attention. He stepped through the door and said, "Then let's pull her out."

With a cup of tasteless coffee from the communal pot, he went to the pilot's flight planning cubicle. After logging on to his favorite aviation website, he checked the weather and filed only the first flight plan of the day to ensure his complete itinerary wouldn't be stored on Air Traffic Control computers. Too many prying eyes out there, and such precautions had unfortunately become a way of life.

Current weather observations and twelve-hour forecasts indicated low clouds and rain for departure and similar conditions in Colorado that evening. Clear weather prevailed over the rest of his route. Good. At least he wouldn't be flying in the murk all day.

He grabbed a copy of the three major newspapers delivered to Schiller every weekday morning and sank down in a soiled armchair in the pilot's lounge. Two articles about the war on terror appeared in the national and world news sections. Neither mentioned his name or the pending investigation, but one followed up yesterday's announcement of a successful attack on the base camp of a recently discovered terrorist "super-cell."

Then the bomb-damage-assessment photos caught his attention. He snatched his reading glasses out of his shirt pocket, slipped them on, and held the page closer to the lamp beside his chair. His heart thudded in his chest. The room seemed to have lost all its oxygen.

He knew that camp. Or what was left of it. Bomb craters the size of small lakes had replaced most of the buildings, but the unique relationship of the river and the road in a figure eight left no doubt. The bastards were shutting the operation down in the only way they knew how.

With trembling hands he folded the papers and set them on the coffee table. The inside of his left wrist began to itch. He rubbed the red, circular patch of fresh skin, took a deep breath and glanced at the muted TV hanging from the ceiling. Behind an immaculately coiffed blonde, film footage from a smart bomb showed the final seconds of a building Larchmont knew only too well.

He vaulted out of the chair, frantically searched the lounge for the remote, gave up, peered at the base of the TV and pressed the volume control. A sliding green bar advanced across the screen in sync with the loudness of the blonde's words, "And this just in, photos from a special forces team on a mop-up operation confirmed the deaths of all twelve terrorists that intelligence reports indicated were operating out of this base camp. We caution you that the following contains graphic images."

Larchmont's knees tried to buckle as he stared at the photos. Bits and pieces of human beings didn't tell him much, but the face of one relatively whole corpse substantiated his worst nightmare. If this guy had died along with eleven others, Larchmont was the single remaining eyewitness to an undertaking best consigned to the shadows. He had just become the clean-up team's next target.

He rushed into the hangar. A jet undergoing inspection dominated more than half of the enormous building. Mechanics had removed instruments, the refreshment center, overhead and side panels, seats, carpet, and floorboards. In addition to the insurance considerations, this display of apparent chaos was the main reason Schiller never allowed customers into maintenance areas. But as an owner-pilot and substantial contributor to Schiller's bottom line, he could ignore NO ADMITTANCE signs with impunity.

Avoiding the clutter around the dismantled jet, he hurried through the hangar to the parking ramp. The main cabin door on his airplane was closed, P.J.'s head visible through the cockpit left side window. Larchmont always flew solo, but the mechanic on his own initiative had taken over many of the preflight duties normally performed by a copilot. He was probably updating navigation charts.

One of the bodyguards approached with Larchmont's rollaboard suitcase. "All done, Mr. Larchmont. Would you like us to go with you?"

Unfortunately, what he would like and what he had to do were like oil and water. "That won't be necessary. I'll let you know my return date and time in the usual way."

The man saluted with a casual wave and departed. Larchmont stowed his luggage in the aft baggage compartment and opened the main cabin door. He climbed in, turned left toward the cockpit and squeezed his 200-plus pounds between the refreshment center and the single aft-facing passenger seat.

P.J. sat on the captain's side with a brown leather binder in his lap. Loose, outdated navigation chart pages lay scattered on the copilot's seat. He slipped an en route map into a plastic sleeve and snapped the binder closed. "There. You're all current. Anything else?"

"No, and I'm in a bit of a hurry." Larchmont backed into the cabin.

P.J. nodded and laid the binder in the copilot's seat. He crumpled the outdated chart pages into a ball, hauled himself out of the cockpit, and paused. One foot on the top step, he looked at Larchmont. "When can I expect—?"

"I'm *really* in a hurry."

"Yes, sir." P.J. stepped onto the ramp and strolled toward the hangar. Larchmont closed and secured the cabin door, checked all six locked-pin indicators, and entered the cockpit. He eased into the left seat and picked up the chart binder to put it on the floor between his seat and the center console. A brown padded mailing envelope lay in the copilot's seat.

Larchmont turned to his left toward the pilot's "foul weather" window. A holdover from earlier days of aviation, the window could be opened from inside the cockpit, even while in flight. He couldn't imagine doing that, but on the ground, it was a convenient feature. He rotated the latch, opened the window and peered out. P.J. stood talking with another mechanic. "Hey, P.J.!"

"Yes, sir?"

"You forgot this." Larchmont held the envelope out the window.

P.J. trotted over and took it. "Sorry, Mr. Larchmont."

"No problem."

After performing his usual abbreviated flight preparations, he started the engines, listened to the current weather, received his clearance, taxied to the active runway and launched into the gray overcast on the first leg of a getaway trip.

Later that evening after two stops, one in Chicago to visit a safe-deposit box, Larchmont filed a flight plan to Denver Centennial Airport. He had no intention of landing there, but the head fake would keep them guessing. To determine his current position, all they needed was his aircraft tail number, and they could monitor his progress on flight tracking websites. Avoiding predictable routines had become a necessity, like water.

About thirty minutes from Denver, he changed his destination to Cedar Valley, Colorado, where his ranch offered a level of security and protection he could not maintain anywhere else. A large staff and a steady stream of guests meant safety in numbers. The watchers would consider this just another of his frequent visits and never suspect that from there he was about to disappear into the sunset. He couldn't wait to bid the bastards farewell.

He glanced around the dim cockpit. His gaze settled for a moment on the right seat, occupied only by his briefcase. More than one person had told him he was crazy to fly single pilot. They said he didn't have the necessary experience and skills, but their doubts and criticisms only made cockpit solitude that much sweeter.

"Golden Nine Two Four Delta Papa, Denver Center, how do you read?"

Why did the controller sound so pissed? Larchmont replied, "Denver, Four Delta Papa reads you loud and clear."

"That's the third call, Four Delta Papa. Expedite descent to and maintain flight level three two zero."

Damn it. This was no time to let his mind wander. He acknowledged the instruction, selected the new flight level in the altitude alerter, programmed the autopilot controller for a 2000-foot-per-minute descent, and eased the throttles back. Denver Center soon cleared him to lower altitude. Passing 28,000 feet, he selected the secondary radio and listened to the automated weather report at Cedar Valley Municipal Airport: winds out of the north at ten knots gusting to fifteen, visibility two miles, with light rain and mist, ceiling 800 feet overcast, temperature six degrees centigrade, dew point four, altimeter 29.75. Typical late fall conditions. Not to be taken lightly, but he'd seen a lot worse.

Cedar Valley Airport had no tower control or terminal radar services. Denver Center would position him for an instrument approach, and once he descended into the valley, he'd lose radio contact. Talk about being on your own. With darkness, mountainous terrain, and poor weather, the time had arrived for some of that precise flying no one else believed he could do.

Shortly after Larchmont leveled the GoldenJet at 9,000 feet, the controller turned him to a heading for intercepting the final course and issued the approach clearance: "Golden Nine Two Four Delta Papa, I show you slightly right of final approach. Maintain niner thousand until established, cleared for the GPS Runway Three Five approach at Cedar Valley. Radar service terminated. Switch to traffic advisory approved. Cancel your flight plan via land line after landing. Good evening."

Although he'd often thought of these moments as cutting the umbilical cord from "Mother Denver," Larchmont had heard these instructions so many times it was almost soothing. He acknowledged, changed the radio to the Cedar Valley frequency, and announced his presence and intentions to any other pilots foolish enough to be flying in this crap. He scanned the cockpit: fuel quantity—good, fuel balance—within limits, fuel cross feed—off, landing V-speeds—calculated and set, cabin pressure—checked and set, recognition lights—on—no, that's way too bright in these clouds, altimeter—29.75, defogger—on high, anti-ice—damn it. What was the temperature at the airport?

He flipped the secondary radio selector switch on to check the weather again and confirmed it was above freezing at the surface. The outside air temperature gauge in the cockpit read one degree below freezing. His airplane had cold-soaked for two hours at 38,000 feet. These were perfect conditions for structural icing, and he hadn't prepared the airplane for it.

His breathing increased as he peered out the side window at the left wing. Couldn't see anything. Turn on the wing inspection light, fool. The light flooded the upper surface of the wing with a brilliant glow, stark white against the blackness. His heart pulsed like an internal exclamation point. Ice coated the leading edge, adding weight and disturbing the airflow over the wing. Even his long-dead grandmother knew that equaled big trouble, and here he was letting it happen.

He had to get that crap off: engine anti-ice switches—on, wing and tail de-ice boots—automatic, windshield heat and defog fan—on. Fan noise and warm air on his face confirmed operation of the defog system. White de-ice boot advisory lights on the annunciator panel lit up to indicate proper cycling, but two sets of amber caution lights told him the engine and wing anti-ice systems weren't working. Why the hell not?

He stared at the lights. Ever since initial training on the GoldenJet, he'd thought the ice-protection systems must have been designed by Rube Goldberg. Lights on meant this, when they went out you knew this, but sometimes they blinked and then you had to guess. Why didn't they work like a toaster? Flip the damn switches on and forget about them?

At this moment, they should have been—hold it—maybe that was normal. Or was it? He struggled to recall the systems diagrams, all those valves opening and closing in the right sequence, and finally remembered that turning the switches on sent hot engine bleed air and electrical power to the surfaces, but the lights wouldn't go out until everything heated up. They'd cycle after that. Okay. Ignore them and fly the jet.

His instrument crosscheck settled into a scan of the attitude and horizontal situation indicators, airspeed, altitude, and descent rate, then after a moment came to an abrupt halt. Something didn't correlate. He concentrated on the moving-map navigation display.

The controller had said he was offset to the right of the final approach course. A correction to intercept the desired track to the runway required a heading to the left of the desired course. The GPS had steered him on a heading in the wrong direction. What the hell was going on?

He keyed the microphone and asked the controller to verify his position. No response. Confusion, then the realization that he'd changed frequencies. A glance at the altimeter—too low for radio contact. Climb and start over?

No. He was tired and had probably misheard the controller. Back to business.

One glance at the annunciator panel to check on the ice protection dried up his throat. The amber caution lights still glowed bright in the darkened cockpit. The damned things were mocking him, laughing, gloating because the wings and engine intakes weren't being kept free of ice. Why not? He stared at the engine turbine speed indicators. *Damn it, Miles.*

At the lower power settings for the approach, the valves diverting hot bleed air to the anti-ice system remained closed. He had to get them open right now.

He lowered the flaps to the approach setting and extended the speed brakes to increase drag, then advanced the throttles to maintain his desired approach speed and get the hot air flowing.

Left hand resting on the yoke and right hand on the throttles, he monitored the autopilot. When it captured the final approach course, he rolled the vertical speed control into a descent and checked the altitude alerter for the next level off at 7,900 feet, the minimum altitude specified until reaching eight miles from the airport.

In his peripheral vision, the amber anti-ice lights flickered, went out. Finally. The tension in his shoulders eased. As he waited for the autopilot to capture the new altitude, he glanced at the approach chart clipped to the yoke to confirm his next altitude restriction and acknowledged the special note:

MOUNTAINOUS TERRAIN ALL QUADRANTS.
USE EXTREME CAUTION DURING PERIODS OF
LOW CEILING AND RESTRICTED VISIBILITY. NIGHT
OPERATIONS NOT RECOMMENDED.

Larchmont appreciated the dangers involved, but he'd flown into Cedar Valley too many times for a little bad weather to shoo him away.

After passing the next navigation fix on the approach, he could descend to 6,400 feet and hold that altitude until three miles from the runway. Only then would it be safe to descend to the minimum altitude authorized, pick up the approach lights and complete the landing.

Then he'd drive to the ranch, take that first sip of River Rock Pale Ale, and sink into his favorite chair with his feet propped on the ottoman in front of a crackling fire. His personal haven. He often fell asleep there and woke up the next morning without a care in the world. At least for a while.

He glanced over his shoulder at the left wing and the fear climbed the back of his neck to the top of his skull. Highlighted against the black night in the pale glow of the inspection light, horizontal streams of water droplets sped by at 130 mph. A thick layer of glistening ice still coated the leading edge. The pneumatic de-ice boots had failed to crack the ice so the slipstream could carry it off the wing. That was probably true of the tail as well, but he had no way of checking it.

How much ice was there? The thickness guide on the leading edge was completely covered up. He'd never seen that much. What next? Abandon the approach and climb through the icing to safety on top of the clouds? How far was it to clear air? After a few seconds he realized it didn't matter. The runway was the closest haven, and with the extra weight of the ice, he could descend easier than he could climb. He hadn't been to church in fifty years, but he muttered a little prayer for divine intervention just in case it might make a difference.

At five miles from the airport, he keyed the microphone button seven times to illuminate the runway lighting system and lowered the landing gear. Four miles from touchdown, he keyed the microphone again and reported his position to no one because every other pilot within radio range had his head on a pillow.

He selected full flaps at three miles, retracted the speed brakes and eased the throttles back to begin his final descent.

The nose pitched up.

He disengaged the autopilot and shoved the yoke forward.

The airplane fought him, airspeed decreasing, the nose trying to pitch up higher. Bewildered, he pushed the throttles forward and with both hands on the yoke tried to regain control.

Suddenly he remembered a cold-weather operations warning not to use full flaps after flying more than ten minutes in continuous icing conditions. He flicked the flap switch to the approach detent. Pressure on the yoke decreased. But the airplane had climbed. He was too high on the descent profile. He yanked the throttles to idle and lowered the nose.

Through the left quarter panel in the glow of the landing lights he caught a brief glimpse of trees . . . where they shouldn't be.

He slammed the throttles forward and hauled back on the yoke. The jet sagged under him, shuddered, clawed for altitude. Stinging beads of sweat fell from his brow into his eyes.

He blinked. The vertical speed indicator became his world, the needle his salvation.

"Climb, you son of a bitch!"

The needle twitched and began to rise just as the jet pitched down and threw Larchmont into the instrument panel and windscreen.

CHAPTER THREE

Nick Phillips wiped the last bit of white haze off the fender of his Porsche Carrera and stepped back to admire the perfect results. If only he had a place to drive it. Bumper-to-bumper creeping in Washington, D.C., was like riding a thoroughbred in a Fourth-of-July parade. He'd probably spent more hours waxing the beast than he had enjoying the feel of it: alive, eager, its headlights peering ahead in vain for some open road. And truth be told, this Saturday morning's love-fest of elbow grease and Carnauba had only been an outlet for nervous energy.

He glanced at his watch and tapped the crystal. As if that would make the hands move any faster, or encourage his wife and daughter to hurry the hell up, go shopping for that *perfect* homecoming dress, and give Nick a little privacy. Laurie wasn't the problem, she knew all about the project from the beginning. Stephanie wouldn't intentionally spoil the surprise, even for her *totally* obnoxious younger brother, but she came into this world curious, missed nothing, and couldn't keep a secret if her life depended on it.

In the back of the garage three boxes lay hidden from prying eyes, filled with hard-to-find special parts for a 1968 Mustang GT 390 Fastback that Nick was restoring as a surprise for Brad's sixteenth birthday. A buddy of Nick's owned a body shop and had agreed to help finish the remaining few items, which were proving the adage that the last 5% of the work on any project worth doing takes 95% of the time.

The kitchen door slammed. Nick looked over his shoulder. Laurie climbed into her new Suburban, parked in the driveway because the two-car garage was dedicated to a workshop and, of course, the Porsche. He glanced at the clearance between his car and the edge of the driveway, mentally fit the Suburban in, decided no way. Not without a safety observer. Less than a month old, Laurie's "tank," as Nick often referred to it, already had a rear-bumper ding, evidence of her touchy-feely method of backing up.

He walked over to the driver's door and tapped on it.

Laurie looked up from programming an address into the navigation system and lowered the window. "Good morning, sweetheart. You were up early."

Nick leaned in. "Couldn't sleep with that human foghorn beside me. How's the tank been working out so far?"

Laurie shrugged. "That foghorn was caught in *your* throat. As for my *vehicle,* I've been thinking I need something even bigger."

"You're joking."

"Not at all. A real tank. The cannon would be really helpful in beltway traffic."

Nick shook his head. He'd best give up. Laurie could banter him to death with his own words. "When is Brad due home?"

"Haven't you learned that he totally rejects the concept of being *due* anywhere?"

"My mistake. When do you expect he will next grace us with his exalted presence?"

"Aha. Something car-sneaky going on?" When Nick nodded, she said, "You probably have until Sunday night."

"Roger that."

Laurie laid her hand on Nick's shoulder. "How are you feeling about this?"

The tear dams in Nick's eyes threatened to break. He coughed, swallowed hard, and looked away.

His father had wanted to rebuild a classic car with Nick for his sixteenth birthday. Death in a plane crash robbed them both of the experience. Although a generation late, this father-son dream would finally be realized in just over two weeks.

Nick wiped the moisture from his eyes. "I wish Dad could be here to see this."

Laurie took Nick's chin gently in her hand and turned his head to face her. "I know you don't believe it, but I think he will be."

The kitchen door slammed again. Stephanie ran up to the car, climbed in the front passenger's seat, and immediately began texting on her smart phone.

Nick looked at Laurie, shook his head, said to Stephanie, "What is it about greeting family members in the morning that you do not understand?"

Her thumbs continued tap-dancing on the screen. "Hi, Dad. Can we go, Mom?"

Nick shrugged. "Yeah, you better rush out there before all the really nice dresses are gone. But don't worry. I hear they have some new burlap fashions over at the Bargain Barn."

Stephanie's thumbs froze above her phone as she fixed Nick with a stare that she had inherited, learned, or otherwise acquired from her mother. "Oooh. Cool. I could do a B-movie cave-woman thing. Low cut, slit way up the side, lots of thigh. Get all those young studs fighting for my favors."

Get out of this while you can, Phillips. When he tried to establish restrictions on the amount of cleavage the real dress would reveal, Laurie set him straight.

"That's my department. All you have to do is make sure the—uh . . . that you take care of that leaking faucet."

Nick smiled. "You drive carefully, dear." He stepped between the Suburban and the Porsche. Laurie managed to back up without running over his toes. Nick waved goodbye and went into the kitchen for a cup of coffee before inspecting the parts. A glance at the muted TV in the breakfast nook stopped him in his tracks. The CNN crawler read: Miles Larchmont killed in the crash of his private jet.

Nick's heart did a double thump. He snatched the digital wired-to-the-world device from the holder clipped to his belt. Ringer volume at maximum. No blinking red light. He was the on-call Investigator-In-Charge of the Aviation "Go" Team. The National Transportation Safety Board Command Center should have notified him immediately. Why didn't they?

He watched a Headline News report. The accident happened last night. If someone had screwed up the notifications, the team was well on its way without a leader. Twenty years' personal experience dealing with government bungling had taught Nick to expect almost anything, but not this. Pick up the phone and scramble the Go Team. How hard can that be?

Nick muted the TV and stared out the kitchen window. Maybe there was a simple explanation. His vacation began in two weeks and covered Brad's birthday and Stephanie's homecoming. Vulnerability for call-out lasted right up to midnight of his final calendar day on duty. To avoid being scrambled on an investigation that would extend into his vacation, he'd arranged for a backup IIC. What if they had done him a favor and replaced him with another lead investigator? Yeah, right.

The NTSB wasn't into favors. No one would automatically make the switch. Scheduling procedures protected both sides of the employment aisle by establishing duty obligations and off-time privileges. There had to be another reason, and for the duty officer to ignore Nick's number-one on-call status meant that someone way above his pay grade had interfered.

The question was, why?

He poured a cup of coffee while he dialed the NTSB Command Center. As the phone began ringing, he paced around the center island. Nervous energy usually flowed out through his feet.

After the duty officer spouted his standard greeting, Nick said, "Why didn't you scramble me on the Larchmont accident?"

"Hello, Nick."

"Has the team been activated?"

"Good morning to you, too."

"Sorry. I'm just in a hurry. What's going on?"

"We got the team scrambling. Looks like it's going to be a big one."

Nick felt as if his feet had just stepped in floor mastic. "What the hell are you talking about? I'm the duty IIC."

"Uh . . . well . . . that may be, but when I'm told to do something, I usually don't argue."

Nick resisted the urge to bite the man's head off. He was only doing his job. "I apologize for barking at you. What happened, please?"

"Director Nordstrom said he'd pick the team leader."

Of course. Nick ended the call and tapped the handset repeatedly into his other palm. The kitchen felt like it was shrinking, collapsing around him, and he wondered if his being replaced might have something to do with the victim.

Like every other American, Nick had been following the controversy for months. Miles Larchmont, veteran of the most successful covert operation in CIA history, had allegedly been recruited to mastermind a secret anti-terrorist campaign. Under his direction, a unit of assassins had roamed around the Middle East, snatched bad boys out of their lairs, and filmed the executions.

The operation remained in the shadows until the beheading of a man later found to be innocent. The video contained inconclusive evidence, but enough to implicate Larchmont, and it left him standing alone above the radar. Justice Department indictments loomed. His public statements threatened to reveal links to the White House, and from there all the way to the Oval Office.

Nick didn't care much for conspiracy theorists who blamed any event they didn't like on government dirty dealing. On the other hand, the arrogance of absolute power frightened him, and his trust of politicians wouldn't fill a thimble. He had regularly visited a new website, larchmontwatch.com, to check up on the latest news, rumor, and fabrication regarding the most notorious name in America. In addition to all the mainstream media attention, the website's core assertion touched a raw nerve:

The government asked Larchmont to help keep us safe from the abomination of global terror. He responded brilliantly, but ultimately allowed patriotism to cloud his judgment and jeopardize the operation. Politically disadvantageous, he became a liability. Rather than own up to what they've done, cowards in the White House abandoned him with denial, and they are content to let him pay the price for their violation of national and international law.

And as of this morning, Larchmont was dead. How convenient. For whom? Who stands to gain the most? That's not a difficult question to answer. The possibility that Larchmont had been eliminated by the very hands that previously patted his back and fed him made Nick's blood run hot.

So, what should he do about it? He could just stay home. Turn off his phone, or like a commercial some years ago about kicking back with a bottle of wine, throw the damn thing as far as he could into a lake. Finish up the Mustang, plan out how he would introduce Brad to his new ride, and get emotionally ready to watch Stephanie be crowned homecoming queen. His little girl. He almost couldn't believe it happened so fast.

But how would turning his back on an unjust world feel as he sat on the sidelines? He pondered that for a few minutes, then hustled upstairs into the study to check the latest on larchmontwatch.com. The site and associated forums looked like they were filling so fast with content they might explode. One article discussed the effect of bombs in airplanes and predicted the investigation would ultimately prove sabotage killed Larchmont. Nick could sit there all day reading and not begin to keep up, but that wouldn't help solve his dilemma. He pushed away from his desk and went back downstairs.

Unsure of his next move, he paced around the kitchen, which felt like a cage. He opened the refrigerator, realized he wasn't hungry, shut the door and stared at the phone. After a few moments he decided to see what his asshole boss had to say.

The infuriating automated phone system at the office put Nick on hold, but his resolve hadn't ebbed one bit by the time he reached Lars Nordstrom, king of the career-obsessed bureaucrats. "What's going on Lars?"

"Uh . . . I'm sitting at my desk and—"

"This isn't a social call, damn it."

"Whoa, Phillips. Last time I checked, you work for me."

Nick almost threw his coffee cup through the kitchen window. He took a deep breath, set the cup down on the counter and shoved his free hand in a jean pocket. "I'm painfully aware of that. I also know the duty IIC gets the first call."

"Don't lecture me on procedure. I wrote the damned book."

A comic book, maybe, titled *Mr. Bumfuck Goes to Washington.* "That's doubtful, but at least we agree on what it says. Why did you replace me?"

Nordstrom sighed, and the earpiece hissed with frustration and impatience. "I didn't. You arranged for a backup."

So that was it. Nordstrom had been snooping around. He probably sent Dickson out to gather intelligence, an oxymoron for sure. "That's between my backup and me."

"Okay. I'll tell the Command Center to call you. Then *you* get the replacement. What I do after that is none of your concern."

"I heard they didn't call me out because you told them not to."

Nordstrom coughed. Nick had worked with him long enough to recognize the signal, a precursor to a well-developed talent for manipulation. The pen-pusher's silky voice oozed out of the earpiece. "I assumed that's what you'd want."

Nick stayed silent, often the best tactic in dealing with Nordstrom. Let him have the floor. The man had a habit of sawing a hole under his feet.

Another cough. "And I want Dickson to get more experience as IIC."

James Dickson was Nordstrom's protégé, even better described as a clone. Political animals both, they'd align themselves with the prevailing winds and never think twice about selling their souls. Nick made his decision as easily as breathing. "Sorry to upset your plans, but I'm taking the investigation. You don't want to fight me on this."

Nordstrom laughed. "And why not, pray tell?"

"Because I'll make a phone call, and an official complaint regarding your blatant favoritism toward Dickson will put the tit of your career in a wringer." Nick held his breath. Gambling wasn't his strong suit, but he was pretty sure Nordstrom had never held a deck of cards, much less played games of chance. *Especially* with his precious career.

After a silent moment, Nordstrom exhaled deeply into the phone. "Okay. Fine. Have it your way."

Nick breathed out as well, hung up and stared out the window above the sink. The garage and the Porsche faded into a haze as his eyes de-focused in thought.

He'd taken a chance, but only a tiny one. Nordstrom's plans to advance to an appointed seat on the Board needed smooth sailing, and supervisors were expected to prevent any turmoil from rising above the surface of bureaucratic tranquility.

And even if his boss had stood his ground, the risk to Nick's career was worth it. No way could he ignore the case being built in the media and on larchmontwatch.com for a high-level government conspiracy of silence. And a Nordstrom-Dickson coalition would be the perfect puppet act for the White House. What better way to arrange a cover-up?

Enlist a couple of government minions eager to please. The investigation would be like dial-a-finding. You want weather to be a factor? Check here. What about pilot error? Fill in this blank. A quick investigation? No problem.

But that was not going to happen on Nick's watch. And to make certain it didn't, he would play two roles during this investigation.

One, official and on the surface, didn't include paying the slightest heed to political controversy. He would investigate this accident in keeping with the single purpose of the NTSB, to determine cause in the name of safety and accident prevention. Period. And if, in the normal course of the inquiry, he discovered any indication that sabotage had played a role in Larchmont's death, he would hand over lead status to the FBI. Then he'd take directions from the Special Agent In Charge. Just like the book said.

In the meantime, unofficially and behind the scenes, he'd examine every piece of that jet with a microscope if that's what it took. And short of falsifying evidence, he was going to prove what he felt in his gut was true. Somebody messed with that airplane to shut Larchmont's mouth for good.

Nick stood up very straight, as if his backbone had just been fused to a steel rod. *They have no idea who they're dealing with.*

He poured his cold coffee into the sink and scrambled upstairs. From his closet he hauled out a large duffel bag prepacked with the basic essentials and spent no more than five minutes shoving clothing into it. After consulting his mental packing list, he grabbed his wool-lined flight jacket off a hanger and dragged the bag to the top of the stairs.

He paused and looked down the hall, an essential part of the departure ritual developed over many years of being on call, never knowing when he'd be ripped away from his family or how long he'd be gone. It was as if he had to absorb as much of *home* as he could before he walked out the door. The connection always leached out of him during investigations no matter how hard he tried to resist it. The search for answers, the importance of the job, and its very personal relationship to Nick's past shoved everything else in life aside.

Light from his son's empty room spilled into the hallway. Nick stepped inside to turn off the reading lamp. A book on muscle cars lay open on the desk, evidence of Brad's fascination with powerful engines and gleaming paint. Nick smiled. He couldn't wait to see his son's face when the cover came off the Mustang.

He glanced at the watch strapped to his left wrist. An old Bulova. His father had been wearing it when he died piloting his airplane. The second hand seemed to be ticking in sync with the beat of Nick's heart. He turned off the lamp and closed Brad's door.

The door to Stephanie's room opened to reveal the environmental disaster his daughter preferred for living space. Along with total rejection of her parents' preference for a neat and tidy house, she had embraced the independence of young adulthood since the age of five.

He took a deep breath. It was as if everything she touched smelled like flowers. As far as he could remember, even changing her diapers—well, that might be going a bit too far. He closed the door and once again stood at the top of the stairs. *I'll miss you guys.* He carried his bags to the garage, called his wife on her cell phone and told her about the trip.

Laurie's voice took on the knife-edged quality she used when she was *not* pleased. "You have got to be kidding me."

Nick swallowed, tried to find moisture for his dry throat. He'd rather walk on bona fide thin ice than do so with Laurie. Whenever she said, *You're on thin ice, Buster,* she meant it, and her tone now carried the message loud and clear. He swallowed again, as ineffectively as the last time. "Listen, I—"

"It's your turn to listen. I was *really* looking forward to this vacation, Nick. I thought you were as well. I guess I was mistaken."

"If you will just let me finish, please?" After a moment of silence, Nick continued, "It's not an either-or deal. The investigation will slow down by Brad's birthday. I'm taking the airplane, so I can make a quick trip back for that. We'll be done before homecoming. You can trust me. I'm going to be here for the kids. Or for me, which is probably more accurate."

"It doesn't matter who you want to be here for. May I remind you of the term *you* love to haul out of your convenient excuses bag? OBE. You remember that one, don't you?"

Sure he did. Overcome by events. It came with the territory, but he wasn't about to say that. He cradled the phone against his shoulder and began cramming the duffels into the Porsche. The ten-pounds-in-a-five-pound-bag saying came to mind. "Look, I'm not making excuses, but I can do a small private jet in my sleep."

"So can that backup investigator you arranged. Let him catnap through this one."

"I . . . I can't do that."

"Why not?"

Nick wanted to recruit Laurie's support for his decision, but he couldn't involve her in the details. How would he do that? Something like: *I'm going out there to conduct a murder investigation, darling. I know that's not my job, but gee, it will be so much more exciting!* Not hardly.

"I'll have to explain later. It'll work out, Laurie, I promise."

"Sorry, but I'm all full up with your promises. Mark my words, Nick. If any of this crap you peddle about the importance of family means anything, you'll plant your ass at home. Since I don't expect to see you this evening, I guess that settles it. See you . . . whenever."

Nick listened to the dead phone for a moment, stuck it in his belt clip and took a deep breath. His mind struggled with the ever-present dilemma: family first; career first; both first, but in sequence.

Ah, yes. That last one, his own special brand of compromise. He'd balanced the tradeoff for years. He could do that again. Couldn't he?

He glanced at the boxes full of Mustang parts. The mechanic could finish it, but—damn. He'd have to come by for the parts. Maybe this afternoon. Or Monday. That would give him enough time. Pay him a nice bonus. Nick called his friend and arranged it.

Ten minutes later, he eased the Porsche out of the driveway for the drive to a small, outlying airport serving the needs of general aviation. Virginia to Colorado, he could be there . . . about noon tomorrow with a stop for the night just before dark and an early launch in the morning. It felt corny to think it, and he couldn't even imagine saying it out loud, but all these years of picking through piles of wreckage for tiny clues couldn't possibly compare with one week of hunting for evidence of murder.

In a room fragrant with the aroma of leather and lemon-polished wood, Lars Nordstrom propped his feet on his massive mahogany desk and sipped a very dry martini. He didn't much care for gin, but many powerful people he knew drank it. And he needed some heavy-duty fortification to help control his temper. He was so mad at Nick Phillips he could barely stand it.

James Dickson lounged in an overstuffed chair on the other side of the desk. He set his Jack Daniel's on a coaster and leaned forward. "I should get going."

Lars glanced at his watch. "You've got time to finish your drink."

Dickson settled back in the chair, which appeared ready to swallow him. "I still don't think Phillips would have filed a complaint. He's got as much to lose as you do."

"You can afford to think whatever you want, but you might remember that it's my coat tails you're hanging onto."

Dickson raised his eyebrows. "How could I forget?"

Lars frowned. What the hell was this? National Day For Underling Rebellion? He felt like slapping the starch out of Dickson but resisted the urge and took another sip of the martini. "I really thought it was going to be easy. He arranged for a backup IIC, so why would he care if you took it?"

"Jesus, Lars. That's a no-brainer. He hates my guts. By the way, how the hell did you find out about his vacation?"

"I'm his boss, in case you've forgotten. The dates are in his personnel records. And I keep this," he held up his fist, forefinger extended, "on the subterranean pulse of the Division. He's restoring a car for his son's birthday, and he's committed to being in town."

Dickson shook his head. "Charging off on an investigation is a strange way to show it."

"You got that right." Lars stared out the window overlooking the greenbelt behind his house and thought about this speed bump in his plans. Phillips was a top-notch investigator, but he wasn't going to be the next Director of the Aviation Division. Dickson, malleable, easy to control, had a lock on the position because Lars had given him the key. This investigation would be perfect for showcasing what the NTSB did for the American public: lights, camera, and action with Dickson at the podium, doing and saying exactly what Lars told him to. But with loose-cannon Phillips grabbing all the publicity, no telling what would happen. The guy had no concept of how to manage perception. He acted like he didn't give a damn, and he probably didn't.

Dickson sipped his bourbon and chased it with Perrier. "Okay, we lost this one. What can go wrong?"

"Plenty. This is aviation." Lars drained his glass and poured another dose of power from a stainless steel mixing cup. From the ice-cold gin he retrieved two olives speared on a yellow cocktail toothpick, pulled off one with his teeth and chewed. He pointed at Dickson with the toothpick and remaining soused olive. "I just got an idea."

Dickson grinned. "Quick. Call the Public Affairs Office."

Lars glared at his favorite gofer, who was very close to being shown the door. "I'm in no mood for any of your crap, James. Stuff a rag in it." When Dickson appeared to sink into the chair with his patented subservient expression and lowered eyes, Lars leaned back, gobbled up the last olive and said, "Here's what I want you to do."

About The Author

Tosh McIntosh's Bachelor of Science degree in Psychology is analogous to the turn signal on a classic, 1960s automobile owned since new by the kind of inconsiderate driver we all love to hate. It's never been used.

Following graduation from the University of Washington in Seattle, Tosh entered the Air Force with the intention of serving a four-year commitment as a pilot before deciding what he really wanted to do with the remainder of his professional life. One ride in a jet trainer consigned that plan to the scrap heap.

Twenty years of flying jet fighters (including two combat tours) remain the highlight of his aviation career. Another twenty years as a commercial airline and corporate pilot and current enjoyment of sport aviation in light aircraft have embedded within him a passion for sharing with others his unique perspective of what it means to be an aviator.

Pilot Error is his first novel in a planned series that will interweave a life-long fascination with writing and thousands of flight hours in pursuit of one goal: to create stories that entertain and put readers up close and personal within his world of the cockpit.

Connect with Tosh online:

http://toshmcintosh.com/

www.ingramcontent.com/pod-product-compliance
Lightning Source LLC
Chambersburg PA
CBHW051446280526
45785CB00003B/1451

9 7 8 1 4 7 7 4 1 5 2 7 6